SUSE Linux Enterprise Server 12 - System Analysis and Tuning Guide

A catalogue record for this book is available from the Hong Kong Public Libraries.

Published in Hong Kong by Samurai Media Limited.

Email: info@samuraimedia.org

ISBN 978-988-8406-53-1

Contents

About This Guide

SUSE Linux Enterprise Server is used for a broad range of usage scenarios in enterprise and scientific data centers. SUSE has ensured SUSE Linux Enterprise Server is set up in a way that it accommodates different operation purposes with optimal performance. However, SUSE Linux Enterprise Server must meet very different demands when employed on a number crunching server compared to a file server, for example.

It is not possible to ship a distribution that is optimized for all workloads. Different workloads vary substantially in some aspects. Most important among those are I/O access patterns, memory access patterns, and process scheduling. A behavior that perfectly suits a certain workload might reduce performance of another workload. For example, I/O-intensive tasks, such as handling database requests, usually have completely different requirements than CPU-intensive tasks, such as video encoding. The versatility of Linux makes it possible to configure your system in a way that it brings out the best in each usage scenario.

This manual introduces you to means to monitor and analyze your system. It describes methods to manage system resources and to tune your system. This guide does *not* offer recipes for special scenarios, because each server has got its own different demands. It rather enables you to thoroughly analyze your servers and make the most out of them.

General Notes on System Tuning

Tuning a system requires a carefully planned proceeding. Learn which steps are necessary to successfully improve your system.

Part II, "System Monitoring"

Linux offers a large variety of tools to monitor almost every aspect of the system. Learn how to use these utilities and how to read and analyze the system log files.

Part III, "Kernel Monitoring"

The Linux kernel itself offers means to examine every nut, bolt and screw of the system. This part introduces you to SystemTap, a scripting language for writing kernel modules that can be used to analyze and filter data. Collect debugging information and find bottlenecks by using kernel probes. Last, monitor applications with the help of Oprofile.

Part IV, "Resource Management"

Learn how to set up a tailor-made system fitting exactly the server's need. Get to know how to use power management while at the same time keeping the performance of a system at a level that matches the current requirements.

The Linux kernel can be optimized either by using sysctl or via the /proc file system. This part covers tuning the I/O performance and optimizing the way how Linux schedules processes. It also describes basic principles of memory management and shows how memory management could be fine-tuned to suit needs of specific applications and usage patterns. Furthermore, it describes how to optimize network performance.

This part enables you to analyze and handle application or system crashes. It introduces tracing tools such as strace or ltrace and describes how to handle system crashes using Kexec and Kdump.

Tip: Getting the SUSE Linux Enterprise SDK

The SDK is a module for SUSE Linux Enterprise and is available via an online channel from the SUSE Customer Center. Alternatively, go to http://download.suse.com/, search for SUSE Linux Enterprise Software Development Kit and download it from there. Refer to *Book "Deployment Guide", Chapter 9 "Installing Modules, Extensions, and Third Party Add-On Products"* for details.

Many chapters in this manual contain links to additional documentation resources. This includes additional documentation that is available on the system and documentation available on the Internet.

For an overview of the documentation available for your product and the latest documentation updates, refer to http://www.suse.com/doc or to the following section:

1 Available Documentation

We provide HTML and PDF versions of our books in different languages. The following manuals for users and administrators are available for this product:

Article "Installation Quick Start"

Lists the system requirements and guides you step-by-step through the installation of SUSE Linux Enterprise Server from DVD, or from an ISO image.

Book "Deployment Guide"

Shows how to install single or multiple systems and how to exploit the product inherent capabilities for a deployment infrastructure. Choose from various approaches, ranging from a local installation or a network installation server to a mass deployment using a remote-controlled, highly-customized, and automated installation technique.

Book "Administration Guide"

Covers system administration tasks like maintaining, monitoring and customizing an initially installed system.

Book "Virtualization Guide"

Describes virtualization technology in general, and introduces libvirt—the unified interface to virtualization—and detailed information on specific hypervisors.

Book "Storage Administration Guide"

Provides information about how to manage storage devices on a SUSE Linux Enterprise Server.

Book "AutoYaST"

AutoYaST is a system for installing one or more SUSE Linux Enterprise systems automatically and without user intervention, using an AutoYaST profile that contains installation and configuration data. The manual guides you through the basic steps of auto-installation: preparation, installation, and configuration.

Book "Security Guide"

Introduces basic concepts of system security, covering both local and network security aspects. Shows how to use the product inherent security software like AppArmor or the auditing system that reliably collects information about any security-relevant events.

Book "Security and Hardening Guide"

Deals with the particulars of installing and setting up a secure SUSE Linux Enterprise Server, and additional post-installation processes required to further secure and harden that installation. Supports the administrator with security-related choices and decisions.

System Analysis and Tuning Guide

An administrator's guide for problem detection, resolution and optimization. Find how to inspect and optimize your system by means of monitoring tools and how to efficiently manage resources. Also contains an overview of common problems and solutions and of additional help and documentation resources.

Book "GNOME User Guide"

Introduces the GNOME desktop of SUSE Linux Enterprise Server. It guides you through using and configuring the desktop and helps you perform key tasks. It is intended mainly for end users who want to make efficient use of GNOME as their default desktop.

Find HTML versions of most product manuals in your installed system under `/usr/share/doc/manual` or in the help centers of your desktop. Find the latest documentation updates at http://www.suse.com/doc where you can download PDF or HTML versions of the manuals for your product.

2 Feedback

Several feedback channels are available:

Bugs and Enhancement Requests

For services and support options available for your product, refer to http://www.suse.com/support/.

To report bugs for a product component, go to https://scc.suse.com/support/requests, log in, and click *Create New*.

User Comments

We want to hear your comments about and suggestions for this manual and the other documentation included with this product. Use the User Comments feature at the bottom of each page in the online documentation or go to http://www.suse.com/doc/feedback.html and enter your comments there.

Mail

For feedback on the documentation of this product, you can also send a mail to `doc-team@suse.de`. Make sure to include the document title, the product version and the publication date of the documentation. To report errors or suggest enhancements, provide a concise description of the problem and refer to the respective section number and page (or URL).

3 Documentation Conventions

The following typographical conventions are used in this manual:

- `/etc/passwd`: directory names and file names

- *placeholder*: replace *placeholder* with the actual value

- `PATH`: the environment variable PATH

- **ls**, `--help`: commands, options, and parameters

- `user`: users or groups

- Alt , Alt – F1 : a key to press or a key combination; keys are shown in uppercase as on a keyboard

- *File, File › Save As*: menu items, buttons

- x86_64 ⟩ This paragraph is only relevant for the x86_64 architecture. The arrows mark the beginning and the end of the text block. ◁
  System z, POWER ⟩ This paragraph is only relevant for the architectures `z Systems` and `POWER`. The arrows mark the beginning and the end of the text block. ◁

- *Dancing Penguins* (Chapter *Penguins*, ↑Another Manual): This is a reference to a chapter in another manual.

I Basics

1 General Notes on System Tuning

This manual discusses how to find the reasons for performance problems and provides means to solve these problems. Before you start tuning your system, you should make sure you have ruled out common problems and have found the cause for the problem. You should also have a detailed plan on how to tune the system, because applying random tuning tips often will not help and could make things worse.

PROCEDURE 1.1: GENERAL APPROACH WHEN TUNING A SYSTEM

1. Specify the problem that needs to be solved.

2. In case the degradation is new, identify any recent changes to the system.

3. Identify why the issue is considered a performance problem.

4. Specify a metric that can be used to analyze performance. This metric could for example be latency, throughput, the maximum number of simultaneously logged-in users, or the maximum number of active users.

5. Measure current performance using the metric from the previous step.

6. Identify the subsystem(s) where the application is spending the most time.

7.
    a. Monitor the system and/or the application.

    b. Analyze the data, categorize where time is being spent.

8. Tune the subsystem identified in the previous step.

9. Remeasure the current performance without monitoring using the same metric as before.

10. If performance is still not acceptable, start over with *Step 3*.

1.1 Be Sure What Problem to Solve

Before starting to tuning a system, try to describe the problem as exactly as possible. A statement like "The system is slow!" is not a helpful problem description. For example, it could make a difference whether the system speed needs to be improved in general or only at peak times.

Furthermore, make sure you can apply a measurement to your problem, otherwise you will not be able to verify if the tuning was a success or not. You should always be able to compare "before" and "after". Which metrics to use depends on the scenario or application you are looking into. Relevant Web server metrics, for example, could be expressed in terms of

Latency

    The time to deliver a page throughput, measured in pages per second or megabytes per second

Active Users

    The maximum number of users that can be downloading pages while still receiving pages within an acceptable latency

1.2 Rule Out Common Problems

A performance problem often is caused by network or hardware problems, bugs, or configuration issues. Make sure to rule out problems such as the ones listed below before attempting to tune your system:

- Check the output of the `systemd` journal (see *Book "Administration Guide", Chapter 10 "*`journalctl`*: Query the* `systemd` *Journal"*) for unusual entries.

- Check (using **top** or **ps**) whether a certain process misbehaves by eating up unusual amounts of CPU time or memory.

- Check for network problems by inspecting `/proc/net/dev`.

- In case of I/O problems with physical disks, make sure it is not caused by hardware problems (check the disk with the `smartmontools`) or by a full disk.

- Ensure that background jobs are scheduled to be carried out in times the server load is low. Those jobs should also run with low priority (set via **nice**).

- If the machine runs several services using the same resources, consider moving services to another server.

- Last, make sure your software is up-to-date.

1.3   Finding the Bottleneck

Finding the bottleneck very often is the hardest part when tuning a system. SUSE Linux Enterprise Server offers many tools to help you with this task. See *Part II, "System Monitoring"* for detailed information on general system monitoring applications and log file analysis. If the problem requires a long-time in-depth analysis, the Linux kernel offers means to perform such analysis. See *Part III, "Kernel Monitoring"* for coverage.

Once you have collected the data, it needs to be analyzed. First, inspect if the server's hardware (memory, CPU, bus) and its I/O capacities (disk, network) are sufficient. If these basic conditions are met, the system might benefit from tuning.

1.4   Step-by-step Tuning

Make sure to carefully plan the tuning itself. It is of vital importance to only do one step at a time. Only by doing so you will be able to measure if the change provided an improvement or even had a negative impact. Each tuning activity should be measured over a sufficient time period to ensure you can do an analysis based on significant data. If you cannot measure a positive effect, do not make the change permanent. Chances are, that it might have a negative effect in the future.

II System Monitoring

2 System Monitoring Utilities

There are number of programs, tools, and utilities which you can use to examine the status of your system. This chapter introduces some and describes their most important and frequently used parameters.

 Note: Gathering and Analyzing System Information with supportconfig

Apart from the utilities presented in the following, SUSE Linux Enterprise Server also contains **supportconfig**, a tool to create reports about the system such as: current Kernel version, hardware, installed packages, partition setup and much more. These reports are used to provide the SUSE support with needed information in case a support ticket is created. However, they can also be analyzed for known issues to help resolve problems faster. For this purpose, SUSE Linux Enterprise Server provides both an appliance and a command line tool for Supportconfig Analysis (SCA). See *Book "Administration Guide", Chapter 36 "Gathering System Information for Support"* for details.

For each of the described commands, examples of the relevant outputs are presented. In the examples, the first line is the command itself (after the tux > or root #). Omissions are indicated with square brackets ([. . .]) and long lines are wrapped where necessary. Line breaks for long lines are indicated by a backslash (\ ).

```
tux > command -x -y
output line 1
output line 2
output line 3 is annoyingly long, so long that \
    we need to break it
output line 4
[...]
output line 98
output line 99
```

The descriptions have been kept short so that we can include as many utilities as possible. Further information for all the commands can be found in the manual pages. Most of the commands also understand the parameter --help, which produces a brief list of possible parameters.

2.1 Multi-Purpose Tools

While most Linux system monitoring tools monitor only a single aspect of the system, there are a few tools with a broader scope. To get an overview and find out which part of the system to examine further, use these tools first.

2.1.1 `vmstat`

vmstat collects information about processes, memory, I/O, interrupts and CPU. If called without a sampling rate, it displays average values since the last reboot. When called with a sampling rate, it displays actual samples:

EXAMPLE 2.1: vmstat OUTPUT ON A LIGHTLY USED MACHINE

```
tux > vmstat 2
procs -----------memory---------- ---swap-- -----io---- -system-- ------cpu-----
 r  b   swpd   free   buff  cache   si   so    bi    bo   in   cs us sy id wa st
 1  0  44264  81520    424 935736    0    0    12    25   27   34  1  0 98  0  0
 0  0  44264  81552    424 935736    0    0     0     0   38   25  0  0 100  0  0
 0  0  44264  81520    424 935732    0    0     0     0   23   15  0  0 100  0  0
 0  0  44264  81520    424 935732    0    0     0     0   36   24  0  0 100  0  0
 0  0  44264  81552    424 935732    0    0     0     0   51   38  0  0 100  0  0
```

EXAMPLE 2.2: vmstat OUTPUT ON A HEAVILY USED MACHINE (CPU BOUND)

```
tux > vmstat 2
procs -----------memory---------- ---swap-- -----io---- -system-- -----cpu------
 r  b   swpd    free   buff   cache   si   so    bi    bo   in   cs us sy id wa st
32  1  26236  459640 110240 6312648    0    0  9944     2 4552 6597 95  5  0  0  0
23  1  26236  396728 110336 6136224    0    0  9588     0 4468 6273 94  6  0  0  0
35  0  26236  554920 110508 6166508    0    0  7684 27992 4474 4700 95  5  0  0  0
28  0  26236  518184 110516 6039996    0    0 10830     4 4446 4670 94  6  0  0  0
21  5  26236  716468 110684 6074872    0    0  8734 20534 4512 4061 96  4  0  0  0
```

> **Tip: First Line of Output**
>
> The first line of the vmstat output always displays average values since the last reboot.

The columns show the following:

r

> Shows the number of processes in the run queue. These processes are waiting for a free CPU slot to be executed. If the number of processes in this column is constantly higher than the number of CPUs available, this is an indication of insufficient CPU power.

b

> Shows the number of processes waiting for a resource other than a CPU. A high number in this column may indicate an I/O problem (network or disk).

swpd

> The amount of swap space (KB) currently used.

free

> The amount of unused memory (KB).

inact

> Recently unused memory that can be reclaimed. This column is only visible when calling **vmstat** with the parameter -a (recommended).

active

> Recently used memory that normally does not get reclaimed. This column is only visible when calling **vmstat** with the parameter -a (recommended).

buff

> File buffer cache (KB) in RAM. This column is not visible when calling **vmstat** with the parameter -a (recommended).

cache

> Page cache (KB) in RAM. This column is not visible when calling **vmstat** with the parameter -a (recommended).

si / so

> Amount of data (KB) that is moved from swap to RAM (si) or from RAM to swap (so) per second. High so values over a long period of time may indicate that an application is leaking memory and the leaked memory is being swapped out. High si values over a long period of time could mean that an application that was inactive for a very long time is now active again. Combined high si and so values for prolonged periods of time are evidence of swap thrashing and may indicate that more RAM needs to be installed in the system because there is not enough memory to hold the working set size.

bi

Number of blocks per second received from a block device (for example, a disk read). Note that swapping also impacts the values shown here.

bo

Number of blocks per second sent to a block device (for example, a disk write). Note that swapping also impacts the values shown here.

in

Interrupts per second. A high value may indicate a high I/O level (network and/or disk), but could also be triggered for other reasons such as inter-processor interrupts triggered by another activity. Make sure to also check `/proc/interrupts` to identify the source of interrupts.

cs

Number of context switches per second. This is the number of times that the kernel replaces executable code of one program in memory with that of another program.

us

Percentage of CPU usage from user processes.

sy

Percentage of CPU usage from system processes.

id

Percentage of CPU time spent idling. If this value is zero over a longer period of time, your CPU(s) are working to full capacity. This is not necessarily a bad sign—rather refer to the values in columns *r* and *b* to determine if your machine is equipped with sufficient CPU power.

wa

If "wa" time is non-zero, it indicates throughput lost because of waiting for I/O. This may be inevitable, for example, if a file is being read for the first time, background writeback cannot keep up, and so on. It can also be an indicator for a hardware bottleneck (network or hard disk). Lastly, it can indicate a potential for tuning the virtual memory manager (refer to *Chapter 14, Tuning the Memory Management Subsystem*).

st

Percentage of CPU time used by virtual machines.

See **vmstat** `--help` for more options.

2.1.2 System Activity Information: **sar**

sar can generate extensive reports on almost all important system activities, among them CPU, memory, IRQ usage, IO, or networking. It can also generate reports on the fly. **sar** gathers all their data from the /proc file system.

 Note: sysstat Package

> **sar** is a part of the sysstat package. You need to install the package either with YaST, or with **zypper in sysstat**.

2.1.2.1 Generating reports with **sar**

To generate reports on the fly, call **sar** with an interval (seconds) and a count. To generate reports from files specify a file name with the option -f instead of interval and count. If file name, interval and count are not specified, **sar** attempts to generate a report from /var/log/sa/sa*DD*, where *DD* stands for the current day. This is the default location to where **sadc** writes its data. Query multiple files with multiple -f options.

```
sar 2 10                          # on-the-fly report, 10 times every 2 seconds
sar -f ~/reports/sar_2014_07_17   # queries file sar_2014_07_17
sar                               # queries file from today in /var/log/sa/
cd /var/log/sa &&\
sar -f sa01 -f sa02               # queries files /var/log/sa/0[12]
```

Find examples for useful **sar** calls and their interpretation below. For detailed information on the meaning of each column, refer to the man (1) of **sar**. Also refer to the man page for more options and reports— **sar** offers plenty of them.

2.1.2.1.1 CPU Usage Report: sar

When called with no options, **sar** shows a basic report about CPU usage. On multi-processor machines, results for all CPUs are summarized. Use the option -P ALL to also see statistics for individual CPUs.

```
root # sar 10 5
Linux 3.12.24-7-default (jupiter)  07/17/14  _x86_64_  (2 CPU)
```

17:51:29	CPU	%user	%nice	%system	%iowait	%steal	%idle
17:51:39	all	57,93	0,00	9,58	1,01	0,00	31,47
17:51:49	all	32,71	0,00	3,79	0,05	0,00	63,45
17:51:59	all	47,23	0,00	3,66	0,00	0,00	49,11
17:52:09	all	53,33	0,00	4,88	0,05	0,00	41,74
17:52:19	all	56,98	0,00	5,65	0,10	0,00	37,27
Average:	all	49,62	0,00	5,51	0,24	0,00	44,62

%iowait displays the percentage of time that the CPU was idle while waiting for an I/O request. If this value is significantly higher than zero over a longer time, there is a bottleneck in the I/O system (network or hard disk). If the *%idle* value is zero over a longer period of time, your CPU is working at capacity.

2.1.2.1.2   Memory Usage Report: sar -r

Generate an overall picture of the system memory (RAM) by using the option -r:

```
root # sar -r 10 5

Linux 3.12.24-7-default (jupiter)  07/17/14  _x86_64_  (2 CPU)
```

17:55:27	kbmemfree	kbmemused	%memused	kbbuffers	kbcached	kbcommit	%commit	kbactive	kbinact	kbdirty
17:55:37	104232	1834624	94.62	20	627340	2677656	66.24	802052	828024	1744
17:55:47	98584	1840272	94.92	20	624536	2693936	66.65	808872	826932	2012
17:55:57	87088	1851768	95.51	20	605288	2706392	66.95	827260	821304	1588
17:56:07	86268	1852588	95.55	20	599240	2739224	67.77	829764	820888	3036
17:56:17	104260	1834596	94.62	20	599864	2730688	67.56	811284	821584	3164
Average:	96086	1842770	95.04	20	611254	2709579	67.03	815846	823746	2309

The columns *kbcommit* and *%commit* show an approximation of the maximum amount of memory (RAM and swap) that the current workload could need. While *kbcommit* displays the absolute number in kilobytes, *%commit* displays a percentage.

2.1.2.1.3   Paging Statistics Report: sar -B

Use the option -B to display the kernel paging statistics.

```
root # sar -B 10 5

Linux 3.12.24-7-default (jupiter)  07/17/14  _x86_64_  (2 CPU)


18:23:01 pgpgin/s pgpgout/s fault/s majflt/s pgfree/s pgscank/s pgscand/s pgsteal/s %vmeff

18:23:11  366.80    11.60  542.50     1.10  4354.80     0.00      0.00      0.00   0.00

18:23:21    0.00   333.30 1522.40     0.00 18132.40     0.00      0.00      0.00   0.00

18:23:31   47.20   127.40 1048.30     0.10 11887.30     0.00      0.00      0.00   0.00

18:23:41   46.40     2.50  336.10     0.10  7945.00     0.00      0.00      0.00   0.00

18:23:51    0.00   583.70 2037.20     0.00 17731.90     0.00      0.00      0.00   0.00

Average:   92.08   211.70 1097.30     0.26 12010.28     0.00      0.00      0.00   0.00
```

The *majflt/s* (major faults per second) column shows how many pages are loaded from disk into memory. The source of the faults may be file accesses or faults. There are times when a large number of major faults are normal such as during application start-up time. If major faults are experienced for the entire lifetime of the application it may be an indication that there is insufficient main memory, particularly if combined with large amounts of direct scanning (pgscand/s).

The *%vmeff* column shows the number of pages scanned (*pgscand/s*) in relation to the ones being reused from the main memory cache or the swap cache (*pgsteal/s*). It is a measurement of the efficiency of page reclaim. Healthy values are either near 100 (every inactive page swapped out is being reused) or 0 (no pages have been scanned). The value should not drop below 30.

2.1.2.1.4   Block Device Statistics Report: sar -d

Use the option -d to display the block device (hard disk, optical drive, USB storage device, etc.). Make sure to use the additional option -p (pretty-print) to make the *DEV* column readable.

```
root # sar -d -p 10 5

 Linux 3.12.24-7-default (jupiter)  07/17/14  _x86_64_  (2 CPU)


18:46:09 DEV   tps rd_sec/s  wr_sec/s  avgrq-sz  avgqu-sz    await    svctm    %util

18:46:19 sda 1.70    33.60      0.00     19.76      0.00     0.47     0.47     0.08

18:46:19 sr0 0.00     0.00      0.00      0.00      0.00     0.00     0.00     0.00
```

```
18:46:19 DEV     tps rd_sec/s  wr_sec/s  avgrq-sz  avgqu-sz    await     svctm     %util
18:46:29 sda    8.60   114.40    518.10     73.55      0.06     7.12      0.93      0.80
18:46:29 sr0    0.00     0.00      0.00      0.00      0.00     0.00      0.00      0.00

18:46:29 DEV     tps rd_sec/s  wr_sec/s  avgrq-sz  avgqu-sz    await     svctm     %util
18:46:39 sda   40.50  3800.80    454.90    105.08      0.36     8.86      0.69      2.80
18:46:39 sr0    0.00     0.00      0.00      0.00      0.00     0.00      0.00      0.00

18:46:39 DEV     tps rd_sec/s  wr_sec/s  avgrq-sz  avgqu-sz    await     svctm     %util
18:46:49 sda    1.40     0.00    204.90    146.36      0.00     0.29      0.29      0.04
18:46:49 sr0    0.00     0.00      0.00      0.00      0.00     0.00      0.00      0.00

18:46:49 DEV     tps rd_sec/s  wr_sec/s  avgrq-sz  avgqu-sz    await     svctm     %util
18:46:59 sda    3.30     0.00    503.80    152.67      0.03     8.12      1.70      0.56
18:46:59 sr0    0.00     0.00      0.00      0.00      0.00     0.00      0.00      0.00

Average: DEV     tps rd_sec/s  wr_sec/s  avgrq-sz  avgqu-sz    await     svctm     %util
Average: sda   11.10   789.76    336.34    101.45      0.09     8.07      0.77      0.86
Average: sr0    0.00     0.00      0.00      0.00      0.00     0.00      0.00      0.00
```

Compare the *Average* values for *tps*, *rd_sec/s*, and *wr_sec/s* of all disks. Constantly high values in the *svctm* and *%util* columns could be an indication that the amount of free space on the disk is insufficient.

If the machine uses multiple disks, then it is best if I/O is interleaved evenly between disks of equal speed and capacity. It will be necessary to take into account whether the storage has multiple tiers. Furthermore, if there are multiple paths to storage then consider what the link saturation will be when balancing how storage is used.

2.1.2.1.5   Network Statistics Reports: sar -n *KEYWORD*

The option -n lets you generate multiple network related reports. Specify one of the following keywords along with the -n:

- *DEV*: Generates a statistic report for all network devices

- *EDEV*: Generates an error statistics report for all network devices

- *NFS*: Generates a statistic report for an NFS client

- *NFSD*: Generates a statistic report for an NFS server

- *SOCK*: Generates a statistic report on sockets

- *ALL*: Generates all network statistic reports

2.1.2.2 Visualizing **sar** Data

sar reports are not always easy to parse for humans. kSar, a Java application visualizing your **sar** data, creates easy-to-read graphs. It can even generate PDF reports. kSar takes data generated on the fly and past data from a file. kSar is licensed under the BSD license and is available from https://sourceforge.net/projects/ksar/.

2.2 System Information

2.2.1 Device Load Information: **iostat**

To monitor the system device load, use **iostat**. It generates reports that can be useful for better balancing the load between physical disks attached to your system.

To be able to use **iostat**, install the package `sysstat`.

The first **iostat** report shows statistics collected since the system was booted. Subsequent reports cover the time since the previous report.

```
tux > iostat
Linux 3.12.24-7-default (jupiter)   29/07/14   _x86_64_  (4 CPU)


avg-cpu:  %user   %nice %system %iowait  %steal   %idle
          17.68    4.49    4.24    0.29    0.00   73.31


Device:           tps    kB_read/s    kB_wrtn/s    kB_read    kB_wrtn
sdb              2.02        36.74        45.73    3544894    4412392
sda              1.05         5.12        13.47     493753    1300276
sdc              0.02         0.14         0.00      13641         37
```

Invoking **iostat** in this way will help you find out whether throughput is different from your expectation, but not why. Such questions can be better answered by an extended report which can be generated by invoking **iostat** -x. Extended reports additionally include, for example, information on average queue sizes and average wait times. Find definitions for each of the displayed column titles in the man page of **iostat** (**man 1 iostat**).

You can also specify that a certain device should be monitored at specified intervals. For example, to generate five reports at three-second intervals for the device sda, use:

```
tux > iostat -p sda 3 5
```

To show statistics of network file systems (NFS), there are two similar utilities:

- **nfsiostat-sysstat** is included with the package sysstat.

- **nfsiostat** is included with the package nfs-client. The option -x shows extended statistics information.

2.2.2   Processor Activity Monitoring: mpstat

The utility **mpstat** examines activities of each available processor. If your system has one processor only, the global average statistics will be reported.

The timing arguments work the same way as with the **iostat** command. Entering **mpstat 2 5** prints five reports for all processors in two-second intervals.

```
root # mpstat 2 5
Linux 3.12.24-7-default (jupiter)   07/18/14   _x86_64_   (2 CPU)


13:51:10  CPU    %usr  %nice  %sys  %iowait  %irq  %soft  %steal  %guest  %gnice   %idle

13:51:12  all    8,27   0,00  0,50     0,00  0,00   0,00    0,00    0,00    0,00   91,23

13:51:14  all   46,62   0,00  3,01     0,00  0,00   0,25    0,00    0,00    0,00   50,13

13:51:16  all   54,71   0,00  3,82     0,00  0,00   0,51    0,00    0,00    0,00   40,97

13:51:18  all   78,77   0,00  5,12     0,00  0,00   0,77    0,00    0,00    0,00   15,35

13:51:20  all   51,65   0,00  4,30     0,00  0,00   0,51    0,00    0,00    0,00   43,54

Average:  all   47,85   0,00  3,34     0,00  0,00   0,40    0,00    0,00    0,00   48,41
```

2.2.3 Task Monitoring: `pidstat`

If you need to see what load a particular task applies to your system, use **pidstat** command. It prints activity of every selected task or all tasks managed by Linux kernel if no task is specified. You can also set the number of reports to be displayed and the time interval between them.

For example, **pidstat** -C firefox 2 3 prints the load statistic for tasks whose command name includes the string "firefox". There will be three reports printed at two second intervals.

```
root # pidstat -C firefox 2 3
Linux 3.12.24-7-default (jupiter)  07/18/14  _x86_64_  (2 CPU)

14:09:11      UID     PID     %usr %system  %guest    %CPU   CPU  Command
14:09:13     1000     387    22,77    0,99    0,00   23,76     1  firefox

14:09:13      UID     PID     %usr %system  %guest    %CPU   CPU  Command
14:09:15     1000     387    46,50    3,00    0,00   49,50     1  firefox

14:09:15      UID     PID     %usr %system  %guest    %CPU   CPU  Command
14:09:17     1000     387    60,50    7,00    0,00   67,50     1  firefox

Average:      UID     PID     %usr %system  %guest    %CPU   CPU  Command
Average:     1000     387    43,19    3,65    0,00   46,84     -  firefox
```

2.2.4 Kernel Ring Buffer: `dmesg`

The Linux kernel keeps certain messages in a ring buffer. To view these messages, enter the command **dmesg -T**.

Older events are logged in the systemd journal. See *Book "Administration Guide", Chapter 10 "journalctl: Query the systemd Journal"* for more information on the journal.

2.2.5   List of Open Files: `lsof`

To view a list of all the files open for the process with process ID *PID*, use `-p`. For example, to view all the files used by the current shell, enter:

```
root # lsof -p $$
COMMAND  PID USER   FD    TYPE DEVICE SIZE/OFF   NODE NAME
bash    8842 root   cwd    DIR   0,32      222   6772 /root
bash    8842 root   rtd    DIR   0,32      166    256 /
bash    8842 root   txt    REG   0,32   656584  31066 /bin/bash
bash    8842 root   mem    REG   0,32  1978832  22993 /lib64/libc-2.19.so
[...]
bash    8842 root    2u    CHR  136,2      0t0      5 /dev/pts/2
bash    8842 root  255u    CHR  136,2      0t0      5 /dev/pts/2
```

The special shell variable `$$`, whose value is the process ID of the shell, has been used.

When used with `-i`, **lsof** lists currently open Internet files as well:

```
root # lsof -i
COMMAND    PID USER   FD   TYPE DEVICE SIZE/OFF NODE NAME
wickedd-d  917 root    8u  IPv4  16627      0t0  UDP *:bootpc
wickedd-d  918 root    8u  IPv6  20752      0t0  UDP [fe80::5054:ff:fe72:5ead]:dhcpv6-client
sshd      3152 root    3u  IPv4  18618      0t0  TCP *:ssh (LISTEN)
sshd      3152 root    4u  IPv6  18620      0t0  TCP *:ssh (LISTEN)
master    4746 root   13u  IPv4  20588      0t0  TCP localhost:smtp (LISTEN)
master    4746 root   14u  IPv6  20589      0t0  TCP localhost:smtp (LISTEN)
sshd      8837 root    5u  IPv4 293709      0t0  TCP jupiter.suse.de:ssh->venus.suse.de:33619 (ESTABLISHED)
sshd      8837 root    9u  IPv6 294830      0t0  TCP localhost:x11 (LISTEN)
sshd      8837 root   10u  IPv4 294831      0t0  TCP localhost:x11 (LISTEN)
```

2.2.6   Kernel and udev Event Sequence Viewer: **udevadm monitor**

udevadm monitor listens to the kernel uevents and events sent out by a udev rule and prints the device path (DEVPATH) of the event to the console. This is a sequence of events while connecting a USB memory stick:

 Note: Monitoring udev Events

Only root user is allowed to monitor udev events by running the **udevadm** command.

```
UEVENT[1138806687] add@/devices/pci0000:00/0000:00:1d.7/usb4/4-2/4-2.2
UEVENT[1138806687] add@/devices/pci0000:00/0000:00:1d.7/usb4/4-2/4-2.2/4-2.2
UEVENT[1138806687] add@/class/scsi_host/host4
UEVENT[1138806687] add@/class/usb_device/usbdev4.10
UDEV   [1138806687] add@/devices/pci0000:00/0000:00:1d.7/usb4/4-2/4-2.2
UDEV   [1138806687] add@/devices/pci0000:00/0000:00:1d.7/usb4/4-2/4-2.2/4-2.2
UDEV   [1138806687] add@/class/scsi_host/host4
UDEV   [1138806687] add@/class/usb_device/usbdev4.10
UEVENT[1138806692] add@/devices/pci0000:00/0000:00:1d.7/usb4/4-2/4-2.2/4-2.2
UEVENT[1138806692] add@/block/sdb
UEVENT[1138806692] add@/class/scsi_generic/sg1
UEVENT[1138806692] add@/class/scsi_device/4:0:0:0
UDEV   [1138806693] add@/devices/pci0000:00/0000:00:1d.7/usb4/4-2/4-2.2/4-2.2
UDEV   [1138806693] add@/class/scsi_generic/sg1
UDEV   [1138806693] add@/class/scsi_device/4:0:0:0
UDEV   [1138806693] add@/block/sdb
UEVENT[1138806694] add@/block/sdb/sdb1
UDEV   [1138806694] add@/block/sdb/sdb1
UEVENT[1138806694] mount@/block/sdb/sdb1
UEVENT[1138806697] umount@/block/sdb/sdb1
```

2.3   Processes

2.3.1   Interprocess Communication: `ipcs`

The command **ipcs** produces a list of the IPC resources currently in use:

```
root # ipcs
------ Message Queues --------
key          msqid       owner       perms       used-bytes    messages

------ Shared Memory Segments --------
key          shmid       owner       perms       bytes        nattch     status
0x00000000 65536         tux         600         524288       2          dest
0x00000000 98305         tux         600         4194304      2          dest
0x00000000 884738        root        600         524288       2          dest
0x00000000 786435        tux         600         4194304      2          dest
0x00000000 12058628      tux         600         524288       2          dest
0x00000000 917509        root        600         524288       2          dest
0x00000000 12353542      tux         600         196608       2          dest
0x00000000 12451847      tux         600         524288       2          dest
0x00000000 11567114      root        600         262144       1          dest
0x00000000 10911763      tux         600         2097152      2          dest
0x00000000 11665429      root        600         2336768      2          dest
0x00000000 11698198      root        600         196608       2          dest
0x00000000 11730967      root        600         524288       2          dest

------ Semaphore Arrays --------
key          semid       owner       perms       nsems
0xa12e0919 32768         tux         666         2
```

2.3.2   Process List: **ps**

The command **ps** produces a list of processes. Most parameters must be written without a minus sign. Refer to **ps --help** for a brief help or to the man page for extensive help.

To list all processes with user and command line information, use **ps axu**:

```
tux > ps axu
```

```
USER       PID %CPU %MEM    VSZ   RSS TTY      STAT START   TIME COMMAND
root         1  0.0  0.3  34376  4608 ?        Ss   Jul24   0:02 /usr/lib/systemd/systemd
root         2  0.0  0.0      0     0 ?        S    Jul24   0:00 [kthreadd]
root         3  0.0  0.0      0     0 ?        S    Jul24   0:00 [ksoftirqd/0]
root         5  0.0  0.0      0     0 ?        S<   Jul24   0:00 [kworker/0:0H]
root         6  0.0  0.0      0     0 ?        S    Jul24   0:00 [kworker/u2:0]
root         7  0.0  0.0      0     0 ?        S    Jul24   0:00 [migration/0]
[...]
tux      12583  0.0  0.1 185980  2720 ?        Sl   10:12   0:00 /usr/lib/gvfs/gvfs-mtp-volume-monitor
tux      12587  0.0  0.1 198132  3044 ?        Sl   10:12   0:00 /usr/lib/gvfs/gvfs-gphoto2-volume-monitor
tux      12591  0.0  0.1 181940  2700 ?        Sl   10:12   0:00 /usr/lib/gvfs/gvfs-goa-volume-monitor
tux      12594  8.1 10.6 1418216 163564 ?      Sl   10:12   0:03 /usr/bin/gnome-shell
tux      12600  0.0  0.3 393448  5972 ?        Sl   10:12   0:00 /usr/lib/gnome-settings-daemon-3.0/gsd-
printer
tux      12625  0.0  0.6 227776 10112 ?        Sl   10:12   0:00 /usr/lib/gnome-control-center-search-
provider
tux      12626  0.5  1.5 890972 23540 ?        Sl   10:12   0:00 /usr/bin/nautilus --no-default-window
[...]
```

To check how many **sshd** processes are running, use the option `-p` together with the command **pidof**, which lists the process IDs of the given processes.

```
tux > ps -p $(pidof sshd)
  PID TTY      STAT   TIME COMMAND
 1545 ?        Ss     0:00 /usr/sbin/sshd -D
 4608 ?        Ss     0:00 sshd: root@pts/0
```

The process list can be formatted according to your needs. The option `-L` returns a list of all keywords. Enter the following command to issue a list of all processes sorted by memory usage:

```
tux > ps ax --format pid,rss,cmd --sort rss
  PID   RSS CMD
  PID   RSS CMD
    2     0 [kthreadd]
    3     0 [ksoftirqd/0]
    4     0 [kworker/0:0]
    5     0 [kworker/0:0H]
```

```
    6      0 [kworker/u2:0]
    7      0 [migration/0]
    8      0 [rcu_bh]
[...]
12518 22996 /usr/lib/gnome-settings-daemon-3.0/gnome-settings-daemon
12626 23540 /usr/bin/nautilus --no-default-window
12305 32188 /usr/bin/Xorg :0 -background none -verbose
12594 164900 /usr/bin/gnome-shell
```

USEFUL ps CALLS

ps aux --sort *column*

> Sort the output by *column*. Replace *column* with
>
> pmem for physical memory ratio
>
> pcpu for CPU ratio
>
> rss for resident set size (non-swapped physical memory)

ps axo pid,%cpu,rss,vsz,args,wchan

> Shows every process, their PID, CPU usage ratio, memory size (resident and virtual), name, and their syscall.

ps axfo pid,args

> Show a process tree.

2.3.3   Process Tree: `pstree`

The command **pstree** produces a list of processes in the form of a tree:

```
tux > pstree
systemd---accounts-daemon---{gdbus}
        |                    |-{gmain}
        |-at-spi-bus-laun---dbus-daemon
        |                     |-{dconf worker}
        |                     |-{gdbus}
        |                     |-{gmain}
        |-at-spi2-registr---{gdbus}
        |-cron
        |-2*[dbus-daemon]
```

```
        |-dbus-launch
        |-dconf-service---{gdbus}
        |               |-{gmain}
        |-gconfd-2
        |-gdm---gdm-simple-slav---Xorg
        |    |                 |-gdm-session-wor---gnome-session---gnome-setti+
        |    |                 |                 |                |-gnome-shell+++
        |    |                 |                 |                |-{dconf work+
        |    |                 |                 |                |-{gdbus}
        |    |                 |                 |                |-{gmain}
        |    |                 |                 |-{gdbus}
        |    |                 |                 |-{gmain}
        |    |                 |-{gdbus}
        |    |                 |-{gmain}
        |    |-{gdbus}
        |    |-{gmain}
[...]
```

The parameter `-p` adds the process ID to a given name. To have the command lines displayed as well, use the `-a` parameter:

2.3.4   Table of Processes: **top**

The command **top** (an abbreviation of "table of processes") displays a list of processes that is refreshed every two seconds. To terminate the program, press ⎡Q⎤. The parameter `-n 1` terminates the program after a single display of the process list. The following is an example output of the command **top -n 1**:

```
tux > top -n 1
Tasks: 128 total,   1 running, 127 sleeping,   0 stopped,   0 zombie
%Cpu(s):  2.4 us,  1.2 sy,  0.0 ni, 96.3 id,  0.1 wa,  0.0 hi,  0.0 si,  0.0 st
KiB Mem:   1535508 total,    699948 used,    835560 free,      880 buffers
KiB Swap:  1541116 total,         0 used,  1541116 free.   377000 cached Mem

  PID USER      PR  NI    VIRT    RES    SHR S  %CPU  %MEM     TIME+ COMMAND
    1 root      20   0  116292   4660   2028 S 0.000 0.303   0:04.45 systemd
```

```
 2 root      20   0       0        0        0 S 0.000 0.000    0:00.00 kthreadd
 3 root      20   0       0        0        0 S 0.000 0.000    0:00.07 ksoftirqd+
 5 root       0 -20       0        0        0 S 0.000 0.000    0:00.00 kworker/0+
 6 root      20   0       0        0        0 S 0.000 0.000    0:00.00 kworker/u+
 7 root      rt   0       0        0        0 S 0.000 0.000    0:00.00 migration+
 8 root      20   0       0        0        0 S 0.000 0.000    0:00.00 rcu_bh
 9 root      20   0       0        0        0 S 0.000 0.000    0:00.24 rcu_sched
10 root      rt   0       0        0        0 S 0.000 0.000    0:00.01 watchdog/0
11 root       0 -20       0        0        0 S 0.000 0.000    0:00.00 khelper
12 root      20   0       0        0        0 S 0.000 0.000    0:00.00 kdevtmpfs
13 root       0 -20       0        0        0 S 0.000 0.000    0:00.00 netns
14 root       0 -20       0        0        0 S 0.000 0.000    0:00.00 writeback
15 root       0 -20       0        0        0 S 0.000 0.000    0:00.00 kintegrit+
16 root       0 -20       0        0        0 S 0.000 0.000    0:00.00 bioset
17 root       0 -20       0        0        0 S 0.000 0.000    0:00.00 crypto
18 root       0 -20       0        0        0 S 0.000 0.000    0:00.00 kblockd
```

By default the output is sorted by CPU usage (column *%CPU*, shortcut ⌗Shift⌗-⌗P⌗). Use the following key combinations to change the sort field:

⌗Shift⌗-⌗M⌗: Resident Memory (*RES*)

⌗Shift⌗-⌗N⌗: Process ID (*PID*)

⌗Shift⌗-⌗T⌗: Time (*TIME+*)

To use any other field for sorting, press ⌗F⌗ and select a field from the list. To toggle the sort order, Use ⌗Shift⌗-⌗R⌗.

The parameter `-U` *UID* monitors only the processes associated with a particular user. Replace *UID* with the user ID of the user. Use **top -U \$(id -u)** to show processes of the current user

2.3.5　z Systems Hypervisor Monitor: **hyptop**

hyptop provides a dynamic real-time view of a z Systems hypervisor environment, using the kernel infrastructure via debugfs. It works with either the z/VM or the LPAR hypervisor. Depending on the available data it, for example, shows CPU and memory consumption of active LPARs or z/VM guests. It provides a curses based user interface similar to the **top** command. **hyptop** provides two windows:

- *sys_list*: Shows a list of systems that the currently hypervisor is running

- *sys*: Shows one system in more detail

You can run **hyptop** in interactive mode (default) or in batch mode with the -b option. Help in the interactive mode is available by pressing ? after **hyptop** is started.

Output for the *sys_list* window under LPAR:

```
12:30:48 | CPU-T: IFL(18) CP(3) UN(3)      ?=help
system  #cpu    cpu    mgm    Cpu+   Mgm+    online
(str)    (#)    (%)    (%)    (hm)   (hm)    (dhm)
H05LP30   10 461.14 10.18 1547:41  8:15 11:05:59
H05LP33    4 133.73  7.57  220:53  6:12 11:05:54
H05LP50    4  99.26  0.01  146:24  0:12 10:04:24
H05LP02    1  99.09  0.00  269:57  0:00 11:05:58
TRX2CFA    1   2.14  0.03    3:24  0:04 11:06:01
H05LP13    6   1.36  0.34    4:23  0:54 11:05:56
TRX1      19   1.22  0.14   13:57  0:22 11:06:01
TRX2      20   1.16  0.11   26:05  0:25 11:06:00
H05LP55    2   0.00  0.00    0:22  0:00 11:05:52
H05LP56    3   0.00  0.00    0:00  0:00 11:05:52
         413 823.39 23.86 3159:57 38:08 11:06:01
```

Output for the "sys_list" window under z/VM:

```
12:32:21 | CPU-T: UN(16)                    ?=help
system  #cpu    cpu    Cpu+    online memuse memmax wcur
(str)    (#)    (%)    (hm)    (dhm)  (GiB)  (GiB)  (#)
T6360004   6 100.31  959:47 53:05:20  1.56   2.00  100
T6360005   2   0.44    1:11  3:02:26  0.42   0.50  100
```

```
T6360014    2   0.27      0:45 10:18:41   0.54    0.75   100
DTCVSW1     1   0.00      0:00 53:16:42   0.01    0.03   100
T6360002    6   0.00    166:26 40:19:18   1.87    2.00   100
OPERATOR    1   0.00      0:00 53:16:42   0.00    0.03   100
T6360008    2   0.00      0:37 30:22:55   0.32    0.75   100
T6360003    6   0.00   3700:57 53:03:09   4.00    4.00   100
NSLCF1      1   0.00      0:02 53:16:41   0.03    0.25   500
EREP        1   0.00      0:00 53:16:42   0.00    0.03   100
PERFSVM     1   0.00      0:53  2:21:12   0.04    0.06     0
TCPIP       1   0.00      0:01 53:16:42   0.01    0.12  3000
DATAMOVE    1   0.00      0:05 53:16:42   0.00    0.03   100
DIRMAINT    1   0.00      0:04 53:16:42   0.01    0.03   100
DTCVSW2     1   0.00      0:00 53:16:42   0.01    0.03   100
RACFVM      1   0.00      0:00 53:16:42   0.01    0.02   100
           75 101.57   5239:47 53:16:42  15.46   22.50  3000
```

Output for the *sys* window under LPAR:

```
14:08:41 | H05LP30 | CPU-T: IFL(18) CP(3) UN(3)           ? = help

cpuid   type    cpu   mgm visual.
(#)     (str)   (%)   (%) (vis)
0        IFL  96.91  1.96 |#######################################  |
1        IFL  81.82  1.46 |###############################          |
2        IFL  88.00  2.43 |#################################        |
3        IFL  92.27  1.29 |#####################################     |
4        IFL  83.32  1.05 |###############################          |
5        IFL  92.46  2.59 |#####################################     |
6        IFL   0.00  0.00 |                                         |
7        IFL   0.00  0.00 |                                         |
8        IFL   0.00  0.00 |                                         |
9        IFL   0.00  0.00 |                                         |
              534.79 10.78
```

Output for the *sys* window under z/VM:

```
15:46:57 | T6360003 | CPU-T: UN(16)              ? = help
cpuid      cpu visual
```

```
(#)        (%) (vis)
0       548.72 |#################################          |
        548.72
```

2.3.6   A top-like I/O Monitor: `iotop`

The **`iotop`** utility displays a table of I/O usage by processes or threads.

 Note: Installing `iotop`

> `iotop` is not installed by default. You need to install it manually with **`zypper in iotop`** as `root`.

`iotop` displays columns for the I/O bandwidth read and written by each process during the sampling period. It also displays the percentage of time the process spent while swapping in and while waiting on I/O. For each process, its I/O priority (class/level) is shown. In addition, the total I/O bandwidth read and written during the sampling period is displayed at the top of the interface.

- The ⬅ and ➡ keys change the sorting.

- R reverses the sort order.

- O toggles between showing all processes and threads (default view) and showing only those doing I/O. (This function is similar to adding `--only` on command line.)

- P toggles between showing threads (default view) and processes. (This function is similar to `--only`.)

- A toggles between showing the current I/O bandwidth (default view) and accumulated I/O operations since **`iotop`** was started. (This function is similar to `--accumulated`.)

- I lets you change the priority of a thread or a process's threads.

- Q quits **`iotop`**.

- Pressing any other key will force a refresh.

Following is an example output of the command `iotop --only`, while `find` and `emacs` are running:

```
tux > iotop --only
Total DISK READ: 50.61 K/s | Total DISK WRITE: 11.68 K/s
  TID  PRIO  USER     DISK READ  DISK WRITE  SWAPIN     IO>    COMMAND
 3416 be/4 tux         50.61 K/s    0.00 B/s  0.00 %   4.05 % find /
  275 be/3 root         0.00 B/s    3.89 K/s  0.00 %   2.34 % [jbd2/sda2-8]
 5055 be/4 tux          0.00 B/s    3.89 K/s  0.00 %   0.04 % emacs
```

`iotop` can be also used in a batch mode (`-b`) and its output stored in a file for later analysis. For a complete set of options, see the manual page (`man 1 iotop`).

2.3.7 Modify a process's niceness: `nice` and `renice`

The kernel determines which processes require more CPU time than others by the process's nice level, also called niceness. The higher the "nice" level of a process is, the less CPU time it will take from other processes. Nice levels range from -20 (the least "nice" level) to 19. Negative values can only be set by `root`.

Adjusting the niceness level is useful when running a non time-critical process that lasts long and uses large amounts of CPU time. For example, compiling a kernel on a system that also performs other tasks. Making such a process "nicer", ensures that the other tasks, for example a Web server, will have a higher priority.

Calling `nice` without any parameters prints the current niceness:

```
tux > nice
0
```

Running `nice` *command* increments the current nice level for the given command by 10. Using `nice` -n *level* *command* lets you specify a new niceness relative to the current one.

To change the niceness of a running process, use `renice` *priority* -p *process id*, for example:

```
renice +5 3266
```

To renice all processes owned by a specific user, use the option `-u user`. Process groups are reniced by the option `-g process group id`.

2.4 Memory

2.4.1 Memory Usage: `free`

The utility **free** examines RAM and swap usage. Details of both free and used memory and swap areas are shown:

```
tux > free
              total        used        free      shared     buffers      cached
Mem:       32900500    32703448      197052           0      255668     5787364
-/+ buffers/cache:     26660416     6240084
Swap:       2046972      304680     1742292
```

The options `-b`, `-k`, `-m`, `-g` show the output in bytes, KB, MB, or GB, respectively. The parameter `-d delay` ensures that the display is refreshed every *delay* seconds. For example, **free -d 1.5** produces an update every 1.5 seconds.

2.4.2 Detailed Memory Usage: `/proc/meminfo`

Use `/proc/meminfo` to get more detailed information on memory usage than with **free**. Actually **free** uses some of the data from this file. See an example output from a 64-bit system below. Note that it slightly differs on 32-bit systems because of different memory management:

```
MemTotal:       1942636 kB
MemFree:        1294352 kB
MemAvailable:   1458744 kB
Buffers:            876 kB
Cached:          278476 kB
SwapCached:           0 kB
Active:          368328 kB
Inactive:        199368 kB
```

```
Active(anon):      288968 kB
Inactive(anon):     10568 kB
Active(file):       79360 kB
Inactive(file):    188800 kB
Unevictable:           80 kB
Mlocked:               80 kB
SwapTotal:        2103292 kB
SwapFree:         2103292 kB
Dirty:                 44 kB
Writeback:              0 kB
AnonPages:         288592 kB
Mapped:             70444 kB
Shmem:              11192 kB
Slab:               40916 kB
SReclaimable:       17712 kB
SUnreclaim:         23204 kB
KernelStack:         2000 kB
PageTables:         10996 kB
NFS_Unstable:           0 kB
Bounce:                 0 kB
WritebackTmp:           0 kB
CommitLimit:      3074608 kB
Committed_AS:     1407208 kB
VmallocTotal:   34359738367 kB
VmallocUsed:       145996 kB
VmallocChunk:   34359588844 kB
HardwareCorrupted:      0 kB
AnonHugePages:      86016 kB
HugePages_Total:        0
HugePages_Free:         0
HugePages_Rsvd:         0
HugePages_Surp:         0
Hugepagesize:        2048 kB
DirectMap4k:        79744 kB
DirectMap2M:      2017280 kB
```

These entries stand for the following:

MemTotal

Total amount of RAM.

MemFree

Amount of unused RAM.

MemAvailable

Estimate of how much memory is available for starting new applications without swapping.

Buffers

File buffer cache in RAM

Cached

Page cache in RAM. This excludes buffer cache and swap cache, but includes *Shmem* memory.

SwapCached

Page cache for swapped-out memory.

Active, Active(anon), Active(file)

Recently used memory that will not be reclaimed unless necessary or on explicit request. *Active* is the sum of *Active(anon)* and *Active(file)*:

- *Active(anon)* tracks swap-backed memory. This includes private and shared anonymous mappings and private file pages after copy-on-write.

- *Active(file)* tracks other file-system backed memory.

Inactive, Inactive(anon), Inactive(file)

Less recently used memory that will usually be reclaimed first. *Inactive* is the sum of *Inactive(anon)* and *Inactive(file)*:

- *Inactive(anon)* tracks swap backed memory. This includes private and shared anonymous mappings and private file pages after copy-on-write.

- *Inactive(file)* tracks other file-system backed memory.

Unevictable

Amount of memory that cannot be reclaimed (for example, because it is *Mlocked* or used as a RAM disk).

Mlocked

Amount of memory that is backed by the `mlock` system call. `mlock` allows processes to define which part of physical RAM their virtual memory should be mapped to. However, `mlock` does not guarantee this placement.

SwapTotal

Amount of swap space.

SwapFree

Amount of unused swap space.

Dirty

Amount of memory waiting to be written to disk, because it contains changes compared to the backing storage.

Writeback

Amount of memory that is currently being written to disk.

Mapped

Memory claimed with the `mmap` system call.

Shmem

Memory shared between groups of processes, such as IPC data, `tmpfs` data and shared anonymous memory.

Slab

Memory allocation for internal data structures of the kernel.

SReclaimable

Slab section that can be reclaimed, such as caches (inode, dentry, etc.).

SUnreclaim

Slab section that cannot be reclaimed.

KernelStack

Amount of kernel space memory used by applications (through system calls).

PageTables

Amount of memory dedicated to page tables of all processes.

NFS_Unstable

NFS pages that have already been sent to the server, but are not yet committed there.

Bounce

Memory used for bounce buffers of block devices.

WritebackTmp

Memory used by FUSE for temporary writeback buffers.

CommitLimit

Amount of memory available to the system based on the overcommit ratio setting. This is only enforced if strict overcommit accounting is enabled.

Committed_AS

An approximation of the total amount of memory (RAM and swap) that the current workload would need in the worst case.

VmallocTotal

Amount of allocated kernel virtual address space.

VmallocUsed

Amount of used kernel virtual address space.

VmallocChunk

The largest contiguous block of available kernel virtual address space.

HardwareCorrupted

Amount of failed memory (can only be detected when using ECC RAM).

AnonHugePages

Anonymous hugepages that are mapped into userspace page tables. These are allocated transparently for processes without being specifically requested, therefore they are also known as *transparent hugepages* (THP).

HugePages_Total

Number of preallocated hugepages for use by `SHM_HUGETLB` and `MAP_HUGETLB` or through the `hugetlbfs` file system, as defined in `/proc/sys/vm/nr_hugepages`

HugePages_Free

Number of hugepages available.

HugePages_Rsvd

Number of hugepages that are committed.

HugePages_Surp

Number of hugepages available beyond *HugePages_Total* ("surplus"), as defined in `/proc/sys/vm/nr_overcommit_hugepages`.

Hugepagesize

Size of a hugepage, on AMD64/Intel 64—the default is 2048 KB.

DirectMap4k **etc.**

Amount of kernel memory that is mapped to pages with a given size (in the example: 4 kB).

2.4.3   Process Memory Usage: smaps

Exactly determining how much memory a certain process is consuming is not possible with standard tools like **top** or **ps**. Use the smaps subsystem, introduced in Kernel 2.6.14, if you need exact data. It can be found at `/proc/`*pid*`/smaps` and shows you the number of clean and dirty memory pages the process with the ID `PID` is using at that time. It differentiates between shared and private memory, so you can see how much memory the process is using without including memory shared with other processes. For more information see `/usr/src/linux/Documentation/filesystems/proc.txt` (requires the package `kernel-source` to be installed).

smaps is expensive to read. Therefore it is not recommended to monitor it regularly, but only when closely monitoring a certain process.

2.5   Networking

 Tip: Traffic Shaping

In case the network bandwidth is lower than expected, you should first check if any traffic shaping rules are active for your network segment.

2.5.1   Basic Network Diagnostics: **ip**

ip is a powerful tool to set up and control network interfaces. You can also use it to quickly view basic statistics about network interfaces of the system. For example, whether the interface is up or how many errors, dropped packets, or packet collisions there are.

If you run **ip** with no additional parameter, it displays a help output. To list all network interfaces, enter **ip addr show** (or abbreviated as **ip a**). **ip addr show up** lists only running network interfaces. **ip -s link show** *device* lists statistics for the specified interface only:

```
root # ip -s link show br0
6: br0: <BROADCAST,MULTICAST,UP,LOWER_UP> mtu 1500 qdisc noqueue state UP mode
 DEFAULT
    link/ether 00:19:d1:72:d4:30 brd ff:ff:ff:ff:ff:ff
    RX: bytes  packets  errors  dropped overrun mcast
    6346104756 9265517  0       10860   0       0
    TX: bytes  packets  errors  dropped carrier collsns
    3996204683 3655523  0       0       0       0
```

ip can also be used to show interfaces (`link`), routing tables (`route`), and much more—refer to **man 8 ip** for details.

```
root # ip route
default via 192.168.2.1 dev eth1
192.168.2.0/24 dev eth0  proto kernel  scope link  src 192.168.2.100
192.168.2.0/24 dev eth1  proto kernel  scope link  src 192.168.2.101
192.168.2.0/24 dev eth2  proto kernel  scope link  src 192.168.2.102
```

```
root # ip link
1: lo: <LOOPBACK,UP,LOWER_UP> mtu 65536 qdisc noqueue state UNKNOWN mode DEFAULT group default
    link/loopback 00:00:00:00:00:00 brd 00:00:00:00:00:00
2: eth0: <BROADCAST,MULTICAST,UP,LOWER_UP> mtu 1500 qdisc pfifo_fast state UP mode DEFAULT group default qlen
 1000
    link/ether 52:54:00:44:30:51 brd ff:ff:ff:ff:ff:ff
3: eth1: <BROADCAST,MULTICAST,UP,LOWER_UP> mtu 1500 qdisc pfifo_fast state UP mode DEFAULT group default qlen
 1000
    link/ether 52:54:00:a3:c1:fb brd ff:ff:ff:ff:ff:ff
4: eth2: <BROADCAST,MULTICAST,UP,LOWER_UP> mtu 1500 qdisc pfifo_fast state UP mode DEFAULT group default qlen
 1000
    link/ether 52:54:00:32:a4:09 brd ff:ff:ff:ff:ff:ff
```

2.5.2 Show the Network Usage of Processes: **nethogs**

In some cases, for example if the network traffic suddenly becomes very high, it is desirable to quickly find out which application(s) is/are causing the traffic. **nethogs**, a tool with a design similar to **top**, shows incoming and outgoing traffic for all relevant processes:

```
PID    USER   PROGRAM                                      DEV   SENT    RECEIVED
27145  root   zypper                                       eth0  5.719   391.749 KB/sec
?      root   ..0:113:80c0:8080:10:160:0:100:30015               0.102     2.326 KB/sec
26635  tux    /usr/lib64/firefox/firefox                   eth0  0.026     0.026 KB/sec
?      root   ..0:113:80c0:8080:10:160:0:100:30045               0.000     0.021 KB/sec
?      root   ..0:113:80c0:8080:10:160:0:100:30045               0.000     0.018 KB/sec
?      root   ..0:113:80c0:8080:10:160:0:100:30015               0.000     0.018 KB/sec
?      root   ..0:113:80c0:8080:10:160:0:100:30045               0.000     0.017 KB/sec
?      root   ..0:113:80c0:8080:10:160:0:100:30045               0.000     0.017 KB/sec
?      root   ..0:113:80c0:8080:10:160:0:100:30045               0.069     0.000 KB/sec
?      root   unknown TCP                                         0.000     0.000 KB/sec

TOTAL                                                             5.916   394.192 KB/sec
```

Like in **top**, **nethogs** features interactive commands:

[M]: cycle between display modes (kb/s, kb, b, mb)

[R]: sort by *RECEIVED*

[S]: sort by *SENT*

[Q]: quit

2.5.3 Ethernet Cards in Detail: ethtool

ethtool can display and change detailed aspects of your Ethernet network device. By default it prints the current setting of the specified device.

```
root # ethtool eth0
Settings for eth0:
 Supported ports: [ TP ]
 Supported link modes:   10baseT/Half 10baseT/Full
                         100baseT/Half 100baseT/Full
```

```
                        1000baseT/Full
  Supports auto-negotiation: Yes
  Advertised link modes:   10baseT/Half 10baseT/Full
                           100baseT/Half 100baseT/Full
                           1000baseT/Full
  Advertised pause frame use: No
  [...]
  Link detected: yes
```

The following table shows **ethtool** options that you can use to query the device for specific information:

ethtool option	**it queries the device for**
-a	pause parameter information
-c	interrupt coalescing information
-g	Rx/Tx (receive/transmit) ring parameter information
-i	associated driver information
-k	offload information
-S	NIC and driver-specific statistics

2.5.4   Show the Network Status: **ss**

ss is a tool to dump socket statistics and replaces the **netstat** command. To show a list of all connections use **ss** parameters:

```
root # ss
Netid  State    Recv-Q Send-Q    Local Address:Port       Peer Address:Port
u_str  ESTAB    0      0                    * 14082                 * 14083
u_str  ESTAB    0      0                    * 18582                 * 18583
u_str  ESTAB    0      0                    * 19449                 * 19450
```

```
u_str    ESTAB    0    0    @/tmp/dbus-gmUUwXABPV 18784         * 18783
u_str    ESTAB    0    0    /var/run/dbus/system_bus_socket 19383 * 19382
u_str    ESTAB    0    0    @/tmp/dbus-gmUUwXABPV 18617         * 18616
u_str    ESTAB    0    0    @/tmp/dbus-58TPPDv8qv 19352         * 19351
u_str    ESTAB    0    0                    * 17658            * 17657
u_str    ESTAB    0    0                    * 17693            * 17694
[..]
```

To show all network ports currently open, use the following command:

```
root # ss -l
Netid  State    Recv-Q Send-Q       Local Address:Port  Peer Address:Port
nl     UNCONN   0      0                 rtnl:4195117              *
nl     UNCONN   0      0       rtnl:wickedd-auto4/811             *
nl     UNCONN   0      0       rtnl:wickedd-dhcp4/813             *
nl     UNCONN   0      0                 rtnl:4195121              *
nl     UNCONN   0      0                 rtnl:4195115              *
nl     UNCONN   0      0       rtnl:wickedd-dhcp6/814             *
nl     UNCONN   0      0                  rtnl:kernel              *
nl     UNCONN   0      0            rtnl:wickedd/817              *
nl     UNCONN   0      0                 rtnl:4195118              *
nl     UNCONN   0      0                rtnl:nscd/706              *
nl     UNCONN   4352   0              tcpdiag:ss/2381             *
[...]
```

When displaying network connections, you can specify the socket type to display: TCP (-t) or UDP (-u) for example. The -p option shows the PID and name of the program to which each socket belongs.

The following example lists all TCP connections and the programs using these connections. The -a option make sure all established connections (listening and non-listening) are shown. The -p option shows the PID and name of the program to which each socket belongs.

```
root # ss -t -a -p
State    Recv-Q Send-Q Local Address:Port    Peer Address:Port
LISTEN   0      128                *:ssh      *:*  users:(("sshd",1551,3))
LISTEN   0      100        127.0.0.1:smtp     *:*  users:(("master",1704,13))
```

```
ESTAB    0    132        10.120.65.198:ssh  10.120.4.150:55715  users:(("sshd",2103,5))

LISTEN   0    128                  :::ssh               :::*   users:(("sshd",1551,4))

LISTEN   0    100              ::1:smtp               :::*   users:(("master",1704,14))
```

2.6 The /proc File System

The /proc file system is a pseudo file system in which the kernel reserves important information in the form of virtual files. For example, display the CPU type with this command:

```
tux > cat /proc/cpuinfo
processor : 0
vendor_id : GenuineIntel
cpu family : 6
model   : 30
model name : Intel(R) Core(TM) i5 CPU        750  @ 2.67GHz
stepping : 5
microcode : 0x6
cpu MHz   : 1197.000
cache size : 8192 KB
physical id : 0
siblings : 4
core id   : 0
cpu cores : 4
apicid   : 0
initial apicid : 0
fpu   : yes
fpu_exception : yes
cpuid level : 11
wp   : yes
flags   : fpu vme de pse tsc msr pae mce cx8 apic sep mtrr pge mca cmov pat pse36
 clflush dts acpi mmx fxsr sse sse2 ss ht tm pbe syscall nx rdtscp lm constant_tsc
 arch_perfmon pebs bts rep_good nopl xtopology nonstop_tsc aperfmperf pni dtes64
 monitor ds_cpl vmx smx est tm2 ssse3 cx16 xtpr pdcm sse4_1 sse4_2 popcnt lahf_lm
 ida dtherm tpr_shadow vnmi flexpriority ept vpid
bogomips : 5333.85
```

```
clflush size : 64
cache_alignment : 64
address sizes : 36 bits physical, 48 bits virtual
power management:
[...]
```

 Tip: Detailed Processor Information

Detailed information about the processor on the x86_64 architecture is also available by running **x86info**.

Query the allocation and use of interrupts with the following command:

```
tux > cat /proc/interrupts
            CPU0        CPU1        CPU2        CPU3
   0:        121           0           0           0   IO-APIC-edge      timer
   8:          0           0           0           1   IO-APIC-edge      rtc0
   9:          0           0           0           0   IO-APIC-fasteoi   acpi
  16:          0       11933           0           0   IO-APIC-fasteoi   ehci_hcd:+
  18:          0           0           0           0   IO-APIC-fasteoi   i801_smbus
  19:          0      117978           0           0   IO-APIC-fasteoi   ata_piix,+
  22:          0           0     3275185           0   IO-APIC-fasteoi   enp5s1
  23:     417927           0           0           0   IO-APIC-fasteoi   ehci_hcd:+
  40:    2727916           0           0           0   HPET_MSI-edge     hpet2
  41:          0     2749134           0           0   HPET_MSI-edge     hpet3
  42:          0           0     2759148           0   HPET_MSI-edge     hpet4
  43:          0           0           0     2678206   HPET_MSI-edge     hpet5
  45:          0           0           0           0   PCI-MSI-edge      aerdrv, P+
  46:          0           0           0           0   PCI-MSI-edge      PCIe PME,+
  47:          0           0           0           0   PCI-MSI-edge      PCIe PME,+
  48:          0           0           0           0   PCI-MSI-edge      PCIe PME,+
  49:          0           0           0         387   PCI-MSI-edge      snd_hda_i+
  50:     933117           0           0           0   PCI-MSI-edge      nvidia
 NMI:       2102        2023        2031        1920   Non-maskable interrupts
 LOC:         92          71          57          41   Local timer interrupts
 SPU:          0           0           0           0   Spurious interrupts
```

```
PMI:        2102      2023      2031      1920   Performance monitoring int+
IWI:       47331     45725     52464     46775   IRQ work interrupts
RTR:           2         0         0         0   APIC ICR read retries
RES:      472911    396463    339792    323820   Rescheduling interrupts
CAL:       48389     47345     54113     50478   Function call interrupts
TLB:       28410     26804     24389     26157   TLB shootdowns
TRM:           0         0         0         0   Thermal event interrupts
THR:           0         0         0         0   Threshold APIC interrupts
MCE:           0         0         0         0   Machine check exceptions
MCP:          40        40        40        40   Machine check polls
ERR:           0
MIS:           0
```

The address assignment of executables and libraries is contained in the maps file:

```
tux > cat /proc/self/maps
08048000-0804c000 r-xp 00000000 03:03 17753        /bin/cat
0804c000-0804d000 rw-p 00004000 03:03 17753        /bin/cat
0804d000-0806e000 rw-p 0804d000 00:00 0            [heap]
b7d27000-b7d5a000 r--p 00000000 03:03 11867        /usr/lib/locale/en_GB.utf8/
b7d5a000-b7e32000 r--p 00000000 03:03 11868        /usr/lib/locale/en_GB.utf8/
b7e32000-b7e33000 rw-p b7e32000 00:00 0
b7e33000-b7f45000 r-xp 00000000 03:03 8837         /lib/libc-2.3.6.so
b7f45000-b7f46000 r--p 00112000 03:03 8837         /lib/libc-2.3.6.so
b7f46000-b7f48000 rw-p 00113000 03:03 8837         /lib/libc-2.3.6.so
b7f48000-b7f4c000 rw-p b7f48000 00:00 0
b7f52000-b7f53000 r--p 00000000 03:03 11842        /usr/lib/locale/en_GB.utf8/
[...]
b7f5b000-b7f61000 r--s 00000000 03:03 9109         /usr/lib/gconv/gconv-module
b7f61000-b7f62000 r--p 00000000 03:03 9720         /usr/lib/locale/en_GB.utf8/
b7f62000-b7f76000 r-xp 00000000 03:03 8828         /lib/ld-2.3.6.so
b7f76000-b7f78000 rw-p 00013000 03:03 8828         /lib/ld-2.3.6.so
bfd61000-bfd76000 rw-p bfd61000 00:00 0            [stack]
ffffe000-fffff000 ---p 00000000 00:00 0            [vdso]
```

A lot more information can be obtained from the /proc file system. Some of the important files and their contents are:

/proc/devices

Available devices

/proc/modules

Kernel modules loaded

/proc/cmdline

Kernel command line

/proc/meminfo

Detailed information about memory usage

/proc/config.gz

gzip-compressed configuration file of the kernel currently running

/proc/PID**/**

Find information about processes currently running in the /proc/NNN directories, where NNN is the process ID (PID) of the relevant process. Every process can find its own characteristics in /proc/self/.

Further information is available in the text file /usr/src/linux/Documentation/filesystems/proc.txt (this file is available when the package kernel-source is installed).

2.6.1 procinfo

Important information from the /proc file system is summarized by the command **procinfo**:

```
tux > procinfo
Linux 3.11.10-17-desktop (geeko@buildhost) (gcc 4.8.1 20130909) #1 4CPU
  [jupiter.example.com]


Memory:      Total       Used       Free     Shared    Buffers     Cached
Mem:       8181908    8000632     181276          0      85472    2850872
Swap:     10481660       1576   10480084


Bootup: Mon Jul 28 09:54:13 2014    Load average: 1.61 0.85 0.74 2/904 25949
```

```
user  :    1:54:41.84  12.7%  page in :    2107312  disk 1:    52212r   20199w
nice  :    0:00:00.46   0.0%  page out:    1714461  disk 2:    19387r   10928w
system:    0:25:38.00   2.8%  page act:     466673  disk 3:      548r      10w
IOwait:    0:04:16.45   0.4%  page dea:     272297
hw irq:    0:00:00.42   0.0%  page flt:  105754526
sw irq:    0:01:26.48   0.1%  swap in :          0
idle  :   12:14:43.65  81.5%  swap out:        394
guest :    0:02:18.59   0.2%
uptime:    3:45:22.24          context :   99809844


irq  0:        121 timer           irq 41:   3238224 hpet3
irq  8:          1 rtc0            irq 42:   3251898 hpet4
irq  9:          0 acpi            irq 43:   3156368 hpet5
irq 16:      14589 ehci_hcd:usb1   irq 45:         0 aerdrv, PCIe PME
irq 18:          0 i801_smbus      irq 46:         0 PCIe PME, pciehp
irq 19:     124861 ata_piix, ata_piix, f irq 47:    0 PCIe PME, pciehp
irq 22:    3742817 enp5s1          irq 48:         0 PCIe PME, pciehp
irq 23:     479248 ehci_hcd:usb2   irq 49:       387 snd_hda_intel
irq 40:    3216894 hpet2           irq 50:   1088673 nvidia
```

To see all the information, use the parameter -a. The parameter -nN produces updates of the information every *N* seconds. In this case, terminate the program by pressing Q.

By default, the cumulative values are displayed. The parameter -d produces the differential values. **procinfo -dn5** displays the values that have changed in the last five seconds:

2.6.2 System Control Parameters: /proc/sys/

System control parameters are used to modify the Linux kernel parameters at runtime. They reside in /proc/sys/ and can be viewed and modified with the sysctl command. To list all parameters, run sysctl -a. A single parameter can be listed with sysctl *parameter name*.

Parameters are grouped into categories and can be listed with sysctl *category* or by listing the contents of the respective directories. The most important categories are listed below. The links to further readings require the installation of the package kernel-source.

sysctl dev (/proc/sys/abi/)

Device-specific information.

sysctl fs (/proc/sys/fs/)

Used file handles, quotas, and other file system-oriented parameters. For details see /usr/src/linux/Documentation/sysctl/fs.txt.

sysctl kernel (/proc/sys/kernel/)

Information about the task scheduler, system shared memory, and other kernel-related parameters. For details see /usr/src/linux/Documentation/sysctl/kernel.txt

systctl net (/proc/sys/net/)

Information about network bridges, and general network parameters (mainly the ipv4/ subdirectory). For details see /usr/src/linux/Documentation/sysctl/net.txt

sysctl vm (/proc/sys/vm/)

Entries in this path relate to information about the virtual memory, swapping, and caching. For details see /usr/src/linux/Documentation/sysctl/vm.txt

To set or change a parameter for the current session, use the command **sysctl** -w *parameter = value*. To permanently change a setting, add a line *parameter = value* to /etc/sysctl.conf.

2.7 Hardware Information

2.7.1 PCI Resources: `lspci`

 Note: Accessing PCI configuration.

Most operating systems require root user privileges to grant access to the computer's PCI configuration.

The command **lspci** lists the PCI resources:

```
root # lspci
00:00.0 Host bridge: Intel Corporation 82845G/GL[Brookdale-G]/GE/PE \
    DRAM Controller/Host-Hub Interface (rev 01)
00:01.0 PCI bridge: Intel Corporation 82845G/GL[Brookdale-G]/GE/PE \
```

```
    Host-to-AGP Bridge (rev 01)
00:1d.0 USB Controller: Intel Corporation 82801DB/DBL/DBM \
    (ICH4/ICH4-L/ICH4-M) USB UHCI Controller #1 (rev 01)
00:1d.1 USB Controller: Intel Corporation 82801DB/DBL/DBM \
    (ICH4/ICH4-L/ICH4-M) USB UHCI Controller #2 (rev 01)
00:1d.2 USB Controller: Intel Corporation 82801DB/DBL/DBM \
    (ICH4/ICH4-L/ICH4-M) USB UHCI Controller #3 (rev 01)
00:1d.7 USB Controller: Intel Corporation 82801DB/DBM \
    (ICH4/ICH4-M) USB2 EHCI Controller (rev 01)
00:1e.0 PCI bridge: Intel Corporation 82801 PCI Bridge (rev 81)
00:1f.0 ISA bridge: Intel Corporation 82801DB/DBL (ICH4/ICH4-L) \
    LPC Interface Bridge (rev 01)
00:1f.1 IDE interface: Intel Corporation 82801DB (ICH4) IDE \
    Controller (rev 01)
00:1f.3 SMBus: Intel Corporation 82801DB/DBL/DBM (ICH4/ICH4-L/ICH4-M) \
    SMBus Controller (rev 01)
00:1f.5 Multimedia audio controller: Intel Corporation 82801DB/DBL/DBM \
    (ICH4/ICH4-L/ICH4-M) AC'97 Audio Controller (rev 01)
01:00.0 VGA compatible controller: Matrox Graphics, Inc. G400/G450 (rev 85)
02:08.0 Ethernet controller: Intel Corporation 82801DB PRO/100 VE (LOM) \
    Ethernet Controller (rev 81)
```

Using `-v` results in a more detailed listing:

```
root # lspci -v
[...]
00:03.0 Ethernet controller: Intel Corporation 82540EM Gigabit Ethernet \
Controller (rev 02)
  Subsystem: Intel Corporation PRO/1000 MT Desktop Adapter
  Flags: bus master, 66MHz, medium devsel, latency 64, IRQ 19
  Memory at f0000000 (32-bit, non-prefetchable) [size=128K]
  I/O ports at d010 [size=8]
  Capabilities: [dc] Power Management version 2
  Capabilities: [e4] PCI-X non-bridge device
  Kernel driver in use: e1000
  Kernel modules: e1000
```

Information about device name resolution is obtained from the file /usr/share/pci.ids. PCI IDs not listed in this file are marked "Unknown device."

The parameter -vv produces all the information that could be queried by the program. To view the pure numeric values, use the parameter -n.

2.7.2 USB Devices: `lsusb`

The command **lsusb** lists all USB devices. With the option -v, print a more detailed list. The detailed information is read from the directory /proc/bus/usb/. The following is the output of **lsusb** with these USB devices attached: hub, memory stick, hard disk and mouse.

```
root # lsusb
Bus 004 Device 007: ID 0ea0:2168 Ours Technology, Inc. Transcend JetFlash \
    2.0 / Astone USB Drive
Bus 004 Device 006: ID 04b4:6830 Cypress Semiconductor Corp. USB-2.0 IDE \
    Adapter
Bus 004 Device 005: ID 05e3:0605 Genesys Logic, Inc.
Bus 004 Device 001: ID 0000:0000
Bus 003 Device 001: ID 0000:0000
Bus 002 Device 001: ID 0000:0000
Bus 001 Device 005: ID 046d:c012 Logitech, Inc. Optical Mouse
Bus 001 Device 001: ID 0000:0000
```

2.7.3 MCELog: Machine Check Exceptions (MCE)

The mcelog package logs and parses/translates Machine Check Exceptions (MCE) on hardware errors (also including memory errors). Formerly this has been done by a cron job executed hourly. Now hardware errors are immediately processed by an mcelog daemon.

However, the mcelog service is not enabled by default, resulting in memory and CPU errors also not being logged by default. In addition, mcelog has a new feature to also handle predictive bad page offlining and automatic core offlining when cache errors happen.

The service can either be enabled and started via the YaST system services editor or via command line:

```
systemctl enable mcelog
```

```
systemctl start mcelog
```

2.8 Files and File Systems

For file system-specific information, refer to *Book* "Storage Administration Guide".

2.8.1 Determine the File Type: `file`

The command **file** determines the type of a file or a list of files by checking `/usr/share/misc/magic`.

```
tux > file /usr/bin/file
/usr/bin/file: ELF 64-bit LSB executable, x86-64, version 1 (SYSV), \
    for GNU/Linux 2.6.4, dynamically linked (uses shared libs), stripped
```

The parameter `-f list` specifies a file with a list of file names to examine. The `-z` allows **file** to look inside compressed files:

```
tux > file /usr/share/man/man1/file.1.gz
/usr/share/man/man1/file.1.gz: gzip compressed data, from Unix, max compression
tux > file -z /usr/share/man/man1/file.1.gz
/usr/share/man/man1/file.1.gz: troff or preprocessor input text \
    (gzip compressed data, from Unix, max compression)
```

The parameter `-i` outputs a mime type string rather than the traditional description.

```
tux > file -i /usr/share/misc/magic
/usr/share/misc/magic: text/plain charset=utf-8
```

2.8.2 File Systems and Their Usage: **mount**, **df** and **du**

The command **mount** shows which file system (device and type) is mounted at which mount point:

```
root # mount
/dev/sda2 on / type ext4 (rw,acl,user_xattr)
```

```
proc on /proc type proc (rw)

sysfs on /sys type sysfs (rw)

debugfs on /sys/kernel/debug type debugfs (rw)

devtmpfs on /dev type devtmpfs (rw,mode=0755)

tmpfs on /dev/shm type tmpfs (rw,mode=1777)

devpts on /dev/pts type devpts (rw,mode=0620,gid=5)

/dev/sda3 on /home type ext3 (rw)

securityfs on /sys/kernel/security type securityfs (rw)

fusectl on /sys/fs/fuse/connections type fusectl (rw)

gvfs-fuse-daemon on /home/tux/.gvfs type fuse.gvfs-fuse-daemon \

(rw,nosuid,nodev,user=tux)
```

Obtain information about total usage of the file systems with the command **df**. The parameter -h (or --human-readable) transforms the output into a form understandable for common users.

```
tux > df -h

Filesystem          Size  Used Avail Use% Mounted on

/dev/sda2            20G  5,9G   13G  32% /

devtmpfs            1,6G  236K  1,6G   1% /dev

tmpfs               1,6G  668K  1,6G   1% /dev/shm

/dev/sda3           208G   40G  159G  20% /home
```

Display the total size of all the files in a given directory and its subdirectories with the command **du**. The parameter -s suppresses the output of detailed information and gives only a total for each argument. -h again transforms the output into a human-readable form:

```
tux > du -sh /opt

192M    /opt
```

2.8.3   Additional Information about ELF Binaries

Read the content of binaries with the **readelf** utility. This even works with ELF files that were built for other hardware architectures:

```
tux > readelf --file-header /bin/ls

ELF Header:

  Magic:   7f 45 4c 46 02 01 01 00 00 00 00 00 00 00 00 00
```

```
Class:                             ELF64
Data:                              2's complement, little endian
Version:                           1 (current)
OS/ABI:                            UNIX - System V
ABI Version:                       0
Type:                              EXEC (Executable file)
Machine:                           Advanced Micro Devices X86-64
Version:                           0x1
Entry point address:               0x402540
Start of program headers:          64 (bytes into file)
Start of section headers:          95720 (bytes into file)
Flags:                             0x0
Size of this header:               64 (bytes)
Size of program headers:           56 (bytes)
Number of program headers:         9
Size of section headers:           64 (bytes)
Number of section headers:         32
Section header string table index: 31
```

2.8.4 File Properties: **stat**

The command **stat** displays file properties:

```
tux > stat /etc/profile
  File: `/etc/profile'
  Size: 9662       Blocks: 24       IO Block: 4096    regular file
Device: 802h/2050d Inode: 132349    Links: 1
Access: (0644/-rw-r--r--) Uid: (    0/    root)  Gid: (    0/    root)
Access: 2009-03-20 07:51:17.000000000 +0100
Modify: 2009-01-08 19:21:14.000000000 +0100
Change: 2009-03-18 12:55:31.000000000 +0100
```

The parameter --file-system produces details of the properties of the file system in which the specified file is located:

```
tux > stat /etc/profile --file-system
```

```
  File: "/etc/profile"
    ID: d4fb76e70b4d1746 Namelen: 255      Type: ext2/ext3
Block size: 4096      Fundamental block size: 4096
Blocks: Total: 2581445   Free: 1717327   Available: 1586197
Inodes: Total: 655776    Free: 490312
```

2.9 User Information

2.9.1 User Accessing Files: fuser

It can be useful to determine what processes or users are currently accessing certain files. Suppose, for example, you want to unmount a file system mounted at /mnt . **umount** returns "device is busy." The command **fuser** can then be used to determine what processes are accessing the device:

```
tux > fuser -v /mnt/*


                  USER        PID ACCESS COMMAND
/mnt/notes.txt    tux      26597 f....  less
```

Following termination of the **less** process, which was running on another terminal, the file system can successfully be unmounted. When used with -k option, **fuser** will terminate processes accessing the file as well.

2.9.2 Who Is Doing What: w

With the command w, find out who is logged onto the system and what each user is doing. For example:

```
tux > w
 16:00:59 up 1 day,  2:41,  3 users,  load average: 0.00, 0.01, 0.05
USER    TTY    FROM         LOGIN@  IDLE  JCPU   PCPU WHAT
tux     :0     console      Wed13   ?xdm?  8:15  0.03s /usr/lib/gdm/gd
```

```
tux      console  :0              Wed13  26:41m  0.00s  0.03s  /usr/lib/gdm/gd
tux      pts/0    :0              Wed13  20:11   0.10s  2.89s  /usr/lib/gnome-
```

If any users of other systems have logged in remotely, the parameter -f shows the computers from which they have established the connection.

2.10 Time and Date

2.10.1 Time Measurement with **time**

Determine the time spent by commands with the **time** utility. This utility is available in two versions: as a Bash built-in and as a program (**/usr/bin/time**).

```
tux >  time find . > /dev/null


real    0m4.051s ❶
user    0m0.042s ❷
sys     0m0.205s ❸
```

❶ The real time that elapsed from the command's start-up until it finished.

❷ CPU time of the user as reported by the times system call.

❸ CPU time of the system as reported by the times system call.

The output of /usr/bin/time is much more detailed. It is recommended to run it with the -v switch to produce human-readable output.

```
/usr/bin/time -v find . > /dev/null
  Command being timed: "find ."
  User time (seconds): 0.24
  System time (seconds): 2.08
  Percent of CPU this job got: 25%
  Elapsed (wall clock) time (h:mm:ss or m:ss): 0:09.03
  Average shared text size (kbytes): 0
  Average unshared data size (kbytes): 0
```

```
Average stack size (kbytes): 0
Average total size (kbytes): 0
Maximum resident set size (kbytes): 2516
Average resident set size (kbytes): 0
Major (requiring I/O) page faults: 0
Minor (reclaiming a frame) page faults: 1564
Voluntary context switches: 36660
Involuntary context switches: 496
Swaps: 0
File system inputs: 0
File system outputs: 0
Socket messages sent: 0
Socket messages received: 0
Signals delivered: 0
Page size (bytes): 4096
Exit status: 0
```

2.11   Graph Your Data: RRDtool

There are a lot of data in the world around you, which can be easily measured in time. For example, changes in the temperature, or the number of data sent or received by your computer's network interface. RRDtool can help you store and visualize such data in detailed and customizable graphs.

RRDtool is available for most Unix platforms and Linux distributions. SUSE® Linux Enterprise Server ships RRDtool as well. Install it either with YaST or by entering

zypper install *rrdtool* in the command line as root.

 Tip: Bindings

> There are Perl, Python, Ruby, and PHP bindings available for RRDtool, so that you can write your own monitoring scripts in your preferred scripting language.

2.11.1 How RRDtool Works

RRDtool is an abbreviation of *Round Robin Database tool. Round Robin* is a method for manipulating with a constant amount of data. It uses the principle of a circular buffer, where there is no end nor beginning to the data row which is being read. RRDtool uses Round Robin Databases to store and read its data.

As mentioned above, RRDtool is designed to work with data that change in time. The ideal case is a sensor which repeatedly reads measured data (like temperature, speed etc.) in constant periods of time, and then exports them in a given format. Such data are perfectly ready for RRDtool, and it is easy to process them and create the desired output.

Sometimes it is not possible to obtain the data automatically and regularly. Their format needs to be preprocessed before it is supplied to RRDtool, and often you need to manipulate RRDtool even manually.

The following is a simple example of basic RRDtool usage. It illustrates all three important phases of the usual RRDtool workflow: *creating* a database, *updating* measured values, and *viewing* the output.

2.11.2 A Practical Example

Suppose we want to collect and view information about the memory usage in the Linux system as it changes in time. To make the example more vivid, we measure the currently free memory over a period of 40 seconds in 4-second intervals. Three applications that usually consume a lot of system memory are started and closed: the Firefox Web browser, the Evolution e-mail client, and the Eclipse development framework.

2.11.2.1 Collecting Data

RRDtool is very often used to measure and visualize network traffic. In such case, the Simple Network Management Protocol (SNMP) is used. This protocol can query network devices for relevant values of their internal counters. Exactly these values are to be stored with RRDtool. For more information on SNMP, see http://www.net-snmp.org/.

Our situation is different—we need to obtain the data manually. A helper script `free_mem.sh` repetitively reads the current state of free memory and writes it to the standard output.

```
tux > cat free_mem.sh
```

```
INTERVAL=4
for steps in {1..10}
do
    DATE=`date +%s`
    FREEMEM=`free -b | grep "Mem" | awk '{ print $4 }'`
    sleep $INTERVAL
    echo "rrdtool update free_mem.rrd $DATE:$FREEMEM"
done
```

- The time interval is set to 4 seconds, and is implemented with the **sleep** command.

- RRDtool accepts time information in a special format - so called *Unix time*. It is defined as the number of seconds since the midnight of January 1, 1970 (UTC). For example, 1272907114 represents 2010-05-03 17:18:34.

- The free memory information is reported in bytes with **free** -b. Prefer to supply basic units (bytes) instead of multiple units (like kilobytes).

- The line with the **echo ...** command contains the future name of the database file (free_mem.rrd), and together creates a command line for updating RRDtool values.

After running **free_mem.sh**, you see an output similar to this:

```
tux > sh free_mem.sh
rrdtool update free_mem.rrd 1272974835:1182994432
rrdtool update free_mem.rrd 1272974839:1162817536
rrdtool update free_mem.rrd 1272974843:1096269824
rrdtool update free_mem.rrd 1272974847:1034219520
rrdtool update free_mem.rrd 1272974851:909438976
rrdtool update free_mem.rrd 1272974855:832454656
rrdtool update free_mem.rrd 1272974859:829120512
rrdtool update free_mem.rrd 1272974863:1180377088
rrdtool update free_mem.rrd 1272974867:1179369472
rrdtool update free_mem.rrd 1272974871:1181806592
```

It is convenient to redirect the command's output to a file with

sh free_mem.sh > free_mem_updates.log

to simplify its future execution.

2.11.2.2 Creating the Database

Create the initial Robin Round database for our example with the following command:

```
tux >  rrdtool create free_mem.rrd --start 1272974834 --step=4 \
DS:memory:GAUGE:600:U:U RRA:AVERAGE:0.5:1:24
```

- This command creates a file called `free_mem.rrd` for storing our measured values in a Round Robin type database.

- The `--start` option specifies the time (in Unix time) when the first value will be added to the database. In this example, it is one less than the first time value of the **free_mem.sh** output (1272974835).

- The `--step` specifies the time interval in seconds with which the measured data will be supplied to the database.

- The `DS:memory:GAUGE:600:U:U` part introduces a new data source for the database. It is called *memory*, its type is *gauge*, the maximum number between two updates is 600 seconds, and the *minimal* and *maximal* value in the measured range are unknown (U).

- `RRA:AVERAGE:0.5:1:24` creates Round Robin archive (RRA) whose stored data are processed with the *consolidation functions* (CF) that calculates the *average* of data points. 3 arguments of the consolidation function are appended to the end of the line .

If no error message is displayed, then `free_mem.rrd` database is created in the current directory:

```
tux > ls -l free_mem.rrd
-rw-r--r-- 1 tux users 776 May  5 12:50 free_mem.rrd
```

2.11.2.3 Updating Database Values

After the database is created, you need to fill it with the measured data. In *Section 2.11.2.1, "Collecting Data"*, we already prepared the file `free_mem_updates.log` which consists of **rrdtool update** commands. These commands do the update of database values for us.

```
tux > sh free_mem_updates.log; ls -l free_mem.rrd
```

A Practical Example

```
-rw-r--r--  1 tux users  776 May  5 13:29 free_mem.rrd
```

As you can see, the size of free_mem.rrd remained the same even after updating its data.

2.11.2.4   Viewing Measured Values

We have already measured the values, created the database, and stored the measured value in it. Now we can play with the database, and retrieve or view its values.

To retrieve all the values from our database, enter the following on the command line:

```
tux > rrdtool fetch free_mem.rrd AVERAGE --start 1272974830 \
--end 1272974871
          memory
1272974832: nan
1272974836: 1.1729059840e+09
1272974840: 1.1461806080e+09
1272974844: 1.0807572480e+09
1272974848: 1.0030243840e+09
1272974852: 8.9019289600e+08
1272974856: 8.3162112000e+08
1272974860: 9.1693465600e+08
1272974864: 1.1801251840e+09
1272974868: 1.1799787520e+09
1272974872: nan
```

POINTS TO NOTICE

- AVERAGE will fetch average value points from the database, because only one data source is defined (*Section 2.11.2.2, "Creating the Database"*) with AVERAGE processing and no other function is available.

- The first line of the output prints the name of the data source as defined in *Section 2.11.2.2, "Creating the Database"*.

- The left results column represents individual points in time, while the right one represents corresponding measured average values in scientific notation.

- The nan in the last line stands for "not a number".

Now a graph representing the values stored in the database is drawn:

```
tux > rrdtool graph free_mem.png \
--start 1272974830 \
--end 1272974871 \
--step=4 \
DEF:free_memory=free_mem.rrd:memory:AVERAGE \
LINE2:free_memory#FF0000 \
--vertical-label "GB" \
--title "Free System Memory in Time" \
--zoom 1.5 \
--x-grid SECOND:1:SECOND:4:SECOND:10:0:%X
```

POINTS TO NOTICE

- `free_mem.png` is the file name of the graph to be created.

- `--start` and `--end` limit the time range within which the graph will be drawn.

- `--step` specifies the time resolution (in seconds) of the graph.

- The `DEF:...` part is a data definition called *free_memory*. Its data are read from the `free_mem.rrd` database and its data source called *memory*. The *average* value points are calculated, because no others were defined in *Section 2.11.2.2, "Creating the Database"*.

- The `LINE...` part specifies properties of the line to be drawn into the graph. It is 2 pixels wide, its data come from the *free_memory* definition, and its color is red.

- `--vertical-label` sets the label to be printed along the *y* axis, and `--title` sets the main label for the whole graph.

- `--zoom` specifies the zoom factor for the graph. This value must be greater than zero.

- `--x-grid` specifies how to draw grid lines and their labels into the graph. Our example places them every second, while major grid lines are placed every 4 seconds. Labels are placed every 10 seconds under the major grid lines.

A Practical Example

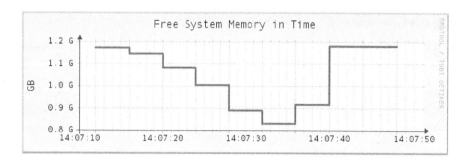

FIGURE 2.1: EXAMPLE GRAPH CREATED WITH RRDTOOL

2.11.3   For More Information

RRDtool is a very complex tool with a lot of sub-commands and command line options. Some are easy to understand, but to make it produce the results you want and fine-tune them according to your liking may require a lot of effort.

Apart from RRDtool's man page (`man 1 rrdtool`) which gives you only basic information, you should have a look at the RRDtool home page [http://oss.oetiker.ch/rrdtool/]. There is a detailed documentation [http://oss.oetiker.ch/rrdtool/doc/index.en.html] of the `rrdtool` command and all its sub-commands. There are also several tutorials [http://oss.oetiker.ch/rrd-tool/tut/index.en.html] to help you understand the common RRDtool workflow.

If you are interested in monitoring network traffic, have a look at MRTG (Multi Router Traffic Grapher) [http://oss.oetiker.ch/mrtg/]. MRTG can graph the activity of many network devices. It can use RRDtool.

3 Analyzing and Managing System Log Files

System log file analysis is one of the most important tasks when analyzing the system. In fact, looking at the system log files should be the first thing to do when maintaining or troubleshooting a system. SUSE Linux Enterprise Server automatically logs almost everything that happens on the system in detail. Since the move to `systemd`, kernel messages and messages of system services registered with `systemd` are logged in `systemd` journal (see *Book "Administration Guide", Chapter 10 "***journalctl***: Query the* `systemd` *Journal"*). Other log files (mainly those of system applications) are written in plain text and can be easily read using an editor or pager. It is also possible to parse them using scripts. This allows you to filter their content.

3.1 System Log Files in `/var/log/`

System log files are always located under the `/var/log` directory. The following list presents an overview of all system log files from SUSE Linux Enterprise Server present after a default installation. Depending on your installation scope, `/var/log` also contains log files from other services and applications not listed here. Some files and directories described below are "placeholders" and are only used, when the corresponding application is installed. Most log files are only visible for the user `root`.

`apparmor`

> AppArmor log files. See *Book "Security Guide"* for details of AppArmor.

`audit`

> Logs from the audit framework. See *Book "Security Guide"* for details.

`ConsoleKit/*`

> Logs of the `ConsoleKit` daemon (daemon for tracking what users are logged in and how they interact with the computer).

`cups/`

> Access and error logs of the Common Unix Printing System (`cups`).

`faillog`

> Database file that contains all login failures. Use the **faillog** command to view. See **man 8 faillog** for more information.

firewall

Firewall logs.

gdm/*

Log files from the GNOME display manager.

krb5

Log files from the Kerberos network authentication system.

lastlog

A database containing information on the last login of each user. Use the command **lastlog** to view. See **man 8 lastlog** for more information.

localmessages

Log messages of some boot scripts, for example the log of the DHCP client.

mail*

Mail server (`postfix`, `sendmail`) logs.

messages

This is the default place where all Kernel and system log messages go and should be the first place (along with `/var/log/warn`) to look at in case of problems.

NetworkManager

NetworkManager log files.

news/*

Log messages from a news server.

ntp

Logs from the Network Time Protocol daemon (`ntpd`).

pk_backend_zypp

PackageKit (with `libzypp` back-end) log files.

puppet/*

Log files from the data center automation tool puppet.

samba/*

Log files from samba, the Windows SMB/CIFS file server.

warn

Log of all system warnings and errors. This should be the first place (along with the output of the `systemd` journal) to look in case of problems.

`wtmp`

Database of all login/logout activities, and remote connections. Use the command **last** to view. See **man 1 last** for more information.

`xinetd.log`

Log files from the extended Internet services daemon (`xinetd`).

`Xorg.0.log`

X.Org start-up log file. Refer to this in case you have problems starting X.Org. Copies from previous X.Org starts are numbered Xorg. *?* .log.

`YaST2/*`

All YaST log files.

`zypp/*`

`libzypp` log files. Refer to these files for the package installation history.

`zypper.log`

Logs from the command line installer **zypper**.

3.2   Viewing and Parsing Log Files

To view log files, you can use any text editor. There is also a simple YaST module for viewing the system log available in the YaST control center under *Miscellaneous* › *System Log*.

For viewing log files in a text console, use the commands **less** or **more**. Use **head** and **tail** to view the beginning or end of a log file. To view entries appended to a log file in real-time use **tail** -f. For information about how to use these tools, see their man pages.

To search for strings or regular expressions in log files use **grep**. **awk** is useful for parsing and rewriting log files.

3.3   Managing Log Files with **logrotate**

Log files under `/var/log` grow on a daily basis and quickly become very large. **logrotate** is a tool that helps you manage log files and their growth. It allows automatic rotation, removal, compression, and mailing of log files. Log files can be handled periodically (daily, weekly, or monthly) or when exceeding a particular size.

logrotate is usually run as a daily `cron` job, and thus usually modifies log files only once a day. However, exceptions occur when a log file is modified because of its size, if **logrotate** is run multiple times a day, or if `--force` is enabled.

The main configuration file of **logrotate** is `/etc/logrotate.conf`. System packages and programs that produce log files (for example, `apache2`) put their own configuration files in the `/etc/logrotate.d/` directory. The content of `/etc/logrotate.d/` is included via `/etc/logrotate.conf`.

EXAMPLE 3.1: EXAMPLE FOR `/etc/logrotate.conf`

```
# see "man logrotate" for details
# rotate log files weekly
weekly


# keep 4 weeks worth of backlogs
rotate 4


# create new (empty) log files after rotating old ones
create


# use date as a suffix of the rotated file
dateext


# uncomment this if you want your log files compressed
#compress


# comment these to switch compression to use gzip or another
# compression scheme
compresscmd /usr/bin/bzip2
uncompresscmd /usr/bin/bunzip2


# RPM packages drop log rotation information into this directory
include /etc/logrotate.d
```

> **!** **Important: Avoid Permission Conflicts**
>
> The `create` option pays heed to the modes and ownerships of files specified in `/etc/permissions*`. If you modify these settings, make sure no conflicts arise.

`logrotate` is controlled through `cron` and is called daily by `/etc/cron.daily/logrotate`. Use `/var/lib/logrotate.status` to find out when a particular file has been rotated lastly.

3.4   Monitoring Log Files with `logwatch`

`logwatch` is a customizable, pluggable log-monitoring script. It parses system logs, extracts the important information and presents them in a human readable manner. To use `logwatch`, install the `logwatch` package.

`logwatch` can either be used at the command line to generate on-the-fly reports, or via `cron` to regularly create custom reports. Reports can either be printed on the screen, saved to a file, or be mailed to a specified address. The latter is especially useful when automatically generating reports via `cron`.

On the command line, you can tell `logwatch` for which service and time span to generate a report and how much detail should be included:

```
# Detailed report on all kernel messages from yesterday
logwatch --service kernel --detail High --range Yesterday --print


# Low detail report on all sshd events recorded (incl. archived logs)
logwatch --service sshd --detail Low --range All --archives --print


# Mail a report on all smartd messages from May 5th to May 7th to root@localhost
logwatch --service smartd --range 'between 5/5/2005 and 5/7/2005' \
--mailto root@localhost --print
```

The `--range` option has got a complex syntax—see `logwatch --range help` for details. A list of all services that can be queried is available with the following command:

```
ls /usr/share/logwatch/default.conf/services/ | sed 's/\.conf//g'
```

`logwatch` can be customized to great detail. However, the default configuration should usually be sufficient. The default configuration files are located under `/usr/share/log-watch/default.conf/`. Never change them because they would get overwritten again with the next update. Rather place custom configuration in `/etc/logwatch/conf/` (you may use the default configuration file as a template, though). A detailed HOWTO on customizing `logwatch` is available at `/usr/share/doc/packages/logwatch/HOWTO-Customize-LogWatch`. The following configuration files exist:

`logwatch.conf`

> The main configuration file. The default version is extensively commented. Each configuration option can be overwritten on the command line.

`ignore.conf`

> Filter for all lines that should globally be ignored by `logwatch`.

`services/*.conf`

> The service directory holds configuration files for each service you can generate a report for.

`logfiles/*.conf`

> Specifications on which log files should be parsed for each service.

3.5 Using **logger** to Make System Log Entries

`logger` is a tool for making entries in the system log. It provides a shell command interface to the rsyslogd system log module. For example, the following line outputs its message in `/var/log/messages` or directly in the journal (if no logging facility is running):

```
logger -t Test "This messages comes from $USER"
```

Depending on the current user and host name, the log contains a line similar to this:

```
Sep 28 13:09:31 venus Test: This messages comes from tux
```

III Kernel Monitoring

4 SystemTap—Filtering and Analyzing System Data

SystemTap provides a command line interface and a scripting language to examine the activities of a running Linux system, particularly the kernel, in fine detail. SystemTap scripts are written in the SystemTap scripting language, are then compiled to C-code kernel modules and inserted into the kernel. The scripts can be designed to extract, filter and summarize data, thus allowing the diagnosis of complex performance problems or functional problems. SystemTap provides information similar to the output of tools like `netstat`, `ps`, `top`, and `iostat`. However, more filtering and analysis options can be used for the collected information.

4.1 Conceptual Overview

Each time you run a SystemTap script, a SystemTap session is started. A number of passes are done on the script before it is allowed to run. Then, the script is compiled into a kernel module and loaded. If the script has been executed before and no system components have changed (for example, different compiler or kernel versions, library paths, or script contents), SystemTap does not compile the script again. Instead, it uses the `*.c` and `*.ko` data stored in the SystemTap cache (`~/.systemtap`). The module is unloaded when the tap has finished running. For an example, see the test run in *Section 4.2, "Installation and Setup"* and the respective explanation.

4.1.1 SystemTap Scripts

SystemTap usage is based on SystemTap scripts (`*.stp`). They tell SystemTap which type of information to collect, and what to do once that information is collected. The scripts are written in the SystemTap scripting language that is similar to AWK and C. For the language definition, see http://sourceware.org/systemtap/langref/. A lot of useful example scripts are available from http://www.sourceware.org/systemtap/examples/.

The essential idea behind a SystemTap script is to name `events`, and to give them `handlers`. When SystemTap runs the script, it monitors for certain events. When an event occurs, the Linux kernel runs the handler as a sub-routine, then resumes. Thus, events serve as the triggers for handlers to run. Handlers can record specified data and print it in a certain manner.

The SystemTap language only uses a few data types (integers, strings, and associative arrays of these), and full control structures (blocks, conditionals, loops, functions). It has a lightweight punctuation (semicolons are optional) and does not need detailed declarations (types are inferred and checked automatically).

For more information about SystemTap scripts and their syntax, refer to *Section 4.3, "Script Syntax"* and to the **stapprobes** and **stapfuncs** man pages, that are available with the `systemtap-docs` package.

4.1.2 Tapsets

Tapsets are a library of prewritten probes and functions that can be used in SystemTap scripts. When a user runs a SystemTap script, SystemTap checks the script's probe events and handlers against the tapset library. SystemTap then loads the corresponding probes and functions before translating the script to C. Like SystemTap scripts themselves, tapsets use the file name extension `*.stp`.

However, unlike SystemTap scripts, tapsets are not meant for direct execution. They constitute the library from which other scripts can pull definitions. Thus, the tapset library is an abstraction layer designed to make it easier for users to define events and functions. Tapsets provide aliases for functions that users could want to specify as an event. Knowing the proper alias is often easier than remembering specific kernel functions that might vary between kernel versions.

4.1.3 Commands and Privileges

The main commands associated with SystemTap are **stap** and **staprun**. To execute them, you either need `root` privileges or must be a member of the `stapdev` or `stapusr` group.

stap

> SystemTap front-end. Runs a SystemTap script (either from file, or from standard input). It translates the script into C code, compiles it, and loads the resulting kernel module into a running Linux kernel. Then, the requested system trace or probe functions are performed.

staprun

> SystemTap back-end. Loads and unloads kernel modules produced by the SystemTap front-end.

For a list of options for each command, use `--help`. For details, refer to the **stap** and the **staprun** man pages.

To avoid giving `root` access to users solely to enable them to work with SystemTap, use one of the following SystemTap groups. They are not available by default on SUSE Linux Enterprise, but you can create the groups and modify the access rights accordingly.

stapdev

> Members of this group can run SystemTap scripts with **stap**, or run SystemTap instrumentation modules with **staprun**. As running **stap** involves compiling scripts into kernel modules and loading them into the kernel, members of this group still have effective `root` access.

stapusr

> Members of this group are only allowed to run SystemTap instrumentation modules with **staprun**. In addition, they can only run those modules from `/lib/modules/kernel_version/systemtap/`. This directory must be owned by `root` and must only be writable for the `root` user.

4.1.4   Important Files and Directories

The following list gives an overview of the SystemTap main files and directories.

`/lib/modules/kernel_version/systemtap/`

> Holds the SystemTap instrumentation modules.

`/usr/share/systemtap/tapset/`

> Holds the standard library of tapsets.

`/usr/share/doc/packages/systemtap/examples`

> Holds several example SystemTap scripts for various purposes. Only available if the `systemtap-docs` package is installed.

`~/.systemtap/cache`

> Data directory for cached SystemTap files.

`/tmp/stap*`

> Temporary directory for SystemTap files, including translated C code and kernel object.

4.2 Installation and Setup

As SystemTap needs information about the kernel, some additional kernel-related packages must be installed. For each kernel you want to probe with SystemTap, you need to install a set of the following packages. This set should exactly match the kernel version and flavor (indicated by `*` in the overview below).

 Important: Repository for Packages with Debugging Information

If you subscribed your system for online updates, you can find "debuginfo" packages in the `*-Debuginfo-Updates` online installation repository relevant for SUSE Linux Enterprise Server 12 SP1. Use YaST to enable the repository.

For the classic SystemTap setup, install the following packages (using either YaST or **zypper**).

- `systemtap`

- `systemtap-server`

- `systemtap-docs` (optional)

- `kernel-*-base`

- `kernel-*-debuginfo`

- `kernel-*-devel`

- `kernel-source-*`

- `gcc`

To get access to the man pages and to a helpful collection of example SystemTap scripts for various purposes, additionally install the `systemtap-docs` package.

To check if all packages are correctly installed on the machine and if SystemTap is ready to use, execute the following command as `root`.

```
stap -v -e 'probe vfs.read {printf("read performed\n"); exit()}'
```

It probes the currently used kernel by running a script and returning an output. If the output is similar to the following, SystemTap is successfully deployed and ready to use:

```
Pass ❶: parsed user script and 59 library script(s) in 80usr/0sys/214real ms.
Pass ❷: analyzed script: 1 probe(s), 11 function(s), 2 embed(s), 1 global(s) in
 140usr/20sys/412real ms.
Pass ❸: translated to C into
 "/tmp/stapDwEk76/stap_1856e21ea1c246da85ad8c66b4338349_4970.c" in 160usr/0sys/408real ms.
Pass ❹: compiled C into "stap_1856e21ea1c246da85ad8c66b4338349_4970.ko" in
 2030usr/360sys/10182real ms.
Pass ❺: starting run.
 read performed
Pass ❺: run completed in 10usr/20sys/257real ms.
```

❶ Checks the script against the existing tapset library in /usr/share/systemtap/tapset/ for any tapsets used. Tapsets are scripts that form a library of pre-written probes and functions that can be used in SystemTap scripts.

❷ Examines the script for its components.

❸ Translates the script to C. Runs the system C compiler to create a kernel module from it. Both the resulting C code (*.c) and the kernel module (*.ko) are stored in the SystemTap cache, ~/.systemtap.

❹ Loads the module and enables all the probes (events and handlers) in the script by hooking into the kernel. The event being probed is a Virtual File System (VFS) read. As the event occurs on any processor, a valid handler is executed (prints the text read performed) and closed with no errors.

❺ After the SystemTap session is terminated, the probes are disabled, and the kernel module is unloaded.

In case any error messages appear during the test, check the output for hints about any missing packages and make sure they are installed correctly. Rebooting and loading the appropriate kernel may also be needed.

4.3 Script Syntax

SystemTap scripts consist of the following two components:

SystemTap Events (Probe Points)
> Name the kernel events at the associated handler should be executed. Examples for events are entering or exiting a certain function, a timer expiring, or starting or terminating a session.

SystemTap Handlers (Probe Body)
> Series of script language statements that specify the work to be done whenever a certain event occurs. This normally includes extracting data from the event context, storing them into internal variables, or printing results.

An event and its corresponding handler is collectively called a `probe`. SystemTap events are also called `probe points`. A probe's handler is also called `probe body`.

Comments can be inserted anywhere in the SystemTap script in various styles: using either `#`, `/* */`, or `//` as marker.

4.3.1 Probe Format

A SystemTap script can have multiple probes. They must be written in the following format:

```
probe event {statements}
```

Each probe has a corresponding statement block. This statement block must be enclosed in `{ }` and contains the statements to be executed per event.

EXAMPLE 4.1: SIMPLE SYSTEMTAP SCRIPT

> The following example shows a simple SystemTap script.
>
> ```
> probe❶ begin❷
> {❸
>     printf❹ ("hello world\n")❺
>     exit ()❻
> }❼
> ```
>
> ❶ Start of the probe.

② Event `begin` (the start of the SystemTap session).

③ Start of the handler definition, indicated by `{`.

④ First function defined in the handler: the `printf` function.

⑤ String to be printed by the `printf` function, followed by a line break (`/n`).

⑥ Second function defined in the handler: the `exit()` function. Note that the System-Tap script will continue to run until the `exit()` function executes. If you want to stop the execution of the script before, stop it manually by pressing `Ctrl`-`C`.

⑦ End of the handler definition, indicated by `}`.

The event `begin` ② (the start of the SystemTap session) triggers the handler enclosed in `{ }`. Here, that is the `printf` function ④. In this case, it prints `hello world` followed by a new line ⑤. Then, the script exits.

If your statement block holds several statements, SystemTap executes these statements in sequence—you do not need to insert special separators or terminators between multiple statements. A statement block can also be nested within another statement blocks. Generally, statement blocks in SystemTap scripts use the same syntax and semantics as in the C programming language.

4.3.2   SystemTap Events (Probe Points)

SystemTap supports several built-in events.

The general event syntax is a dotted-symbol sequence. This allows a breakdown of the event namespace into parts. Each component identifier may be parametrized by a string or number literal, with a syntax like a function call. A component may include a `*` character, to expand to other matching probe points. A probe point may be followed by a `?` character, to indicate that it is optional, and that no error should result if it fails to expand. Alternately, a probe point may be followed by a `!` character to indicate that it is both optional and sufficient.

SystemTap supports multiple events per probe—they need to be separated by a comma (`,`). If multiple events are specified in a single probe, SystemTap will execute the handler when any of the specified events occur.

In general, events can be classified into the following categories:

* Synchronous events: Occur when any process executes an instruction at a particular location in kernel code. This gives other events a reference point (instruction address) from which more contextual data may be available.

An example for a synchronous event is `vfs.file_operation`: The entry to the `file_operation` event for Virtual File System (VFS). For example, in *Section 4.2, "Installation and Setup"*, `read` is the `file_operation` event used for VFS.

- Asynchronous events: Not tied to a particular instruction or location in code. This family of probe points consists mainly of counters, timers, and similar constructs.

  Examples for asynchronous events are: `begin` (start of a SystemTap session—as soon as a SystemTap script is run, `end` (end of a SystemTap session), or timer events. Timer events specify a handler to be executed periodically, like `example timer.s(seconds)`, or `timer.ms(milliseconds)`.

  When used in conjunction with other probes that collect information, timer events allow you to print out periodic updates and see how that information changes over time.

EXAMPLE 4.2: PROBE WITH TIMER EVENT

For example, the following probe would print the text "hello world" every 4 seconds:

```
probe timer.s(4)
{
    printf("hello world\n")
}
```

For detailed information about supported events, refer to the **stapprobes** man page. The *See Also* section of the man page also contains links to other man pages that discuss supported events for specific subsystems and components.

4.3.3   SystemTap Handlers (Probe Body)

Each SystemTap event is accompanied by a corresponding handler defined for that event, consisting of a statement block.

4.3.3.1   Functions

If you need the same set of statements in multiple probes, you can place them in a function for easy reuse. Functions are defined by the keyword `function` followed by a name. They take any number of string or numeric arguments (by value) and may return a single string or number.

```
function function_name(arguments) {statements}
probe event {function_name(arguments)}
```

The statements in *function_name* are executed when the probe for *event* executes. The *arguments* are optional values passed into the function.

Functions can be defined anywhere in the script. They may take any

One of the functions needed very often was already introduced in *Example 4.1, "Simple SystemTap Script"*: the `printf` function for printing data in a formatted way. When using the `printf` function, you can specify how arguments should be printed by using a format string. The format string is included in quotation marks and can contain further format specifiers, introduced by a `%` character.

Which format strings to use depends on your list of arguments. Format strings can have multiple format specifiers—each matching a corresponding argument. Multiple arguments can be separated by a comma.

EXAMPLE 4.3: `printf` **FUNCTION WITH FORMAT SPECIFIERS**

```
printf ("❶%s❷(%d❸) open\n❹", execname(), pid())
```

❶ Start of the format string, indicated by `"`.

❷ String format specifier.

❸ Integer format specifier.

❹ End of the format string, indicated by `"`.

The example above prints the current executable name (`execname()`) as a string and the process ID (`pid()`) as an integer in brackets. Then, a space, the word open and a line break follow:

```
[...]
vmware-guestd(2206) open
hald(2360) open
[...]
```

Apart from the two functions `execname()` and `pid()` used in *Example 4.3, "`printf` Function with Format Specifiers"*, a variety of other functions can be used as `printf` arguments.

Among the most commonly used SystemTap functions are the following:

tid()

ID of the current thread.

pid()

Process ID of the current thread.

uId()

ID of the current user.

cpu()

Current CPU number.

execname()

Name of the current process.

gettimeofday_s()

Number of seconds since Unix epoch (January 1, 1970).

ctime()

Convert time into a string.

pp()

String describing the probe point currently being handled.

thread_indent()

Useful function for organizing print results. It (internally) stores an indentation counter for each thread (`tid()`). The function takes one argument, an indentation delta, indicating how many spaces to add or remove from the thread's indentation counter. It returns a string with some generic trace data along with an appropriate number of indentation spaces. The generic data returned includes a time stamp (number of microseconds since the initial indentation for the thread), a process name, and the thread ID itself. This allows you to identify what functions were called, who called them, and how long they took.

Call entries and exits often do not immediately precede each other (otherwise it would be easy to match them). In between a first call entry and its exit, usually a number of other call entries and exits are made. The indentation counter helps you match an entry with its corresponding exit as it indents the next function call in case it is *not* the exit of the previous one. For an example SystemTap script using `thread_indent()` and the respective output, refer to the *SystemTap Tutorial*: http://sourceware.org/systemtap/tutorial/Tracing.html#fig:socket-trace.

For more information about supported SystemTap functions, refer to the **stapfuncs** man page.

4.3.3.2 Other Basic Constructs

Apart from functions, you can use several other common constructs in SystemTap handlers, including variables, conditional statements (like `if`/`else`, `while` loops, `for` loops, arrays or command line arguments.

4.3.3.2.1 Variables

Variables may be defined anywhere in the script. To define one, simply choose a name and assign a value from a function or expression to it:

```
foo = gettimeofday( )
```

Then you can use the variable in an expression. From the type of values assigned to the variable, SystemTap automatically infers the type of each identifier (string or number). Any inconsistencies will be reported as errors. In the example above, `foo` would automatically be classified as a number and could be printed via `printf()` with the integer format specifier (`%d`).

However, by default, variables are local to the probe they are used in: They are initialized, used and disposed of at each handler evocation. To share variables between probes, declare them global anywhere in the script. To do so, use the `global` keyword outside of the probes:

EXAMPLE 4.4: USING GLOBAL VARIABLES

```
global count_jiffies, count_ms
probe timer.jiffies(100) { count_jiffies ++ }
probe timer.ms(100) { count_ms ++ }
probe timer.ms(12345)
{
  hz=(1000*count_jiffies) / count_ms
  printf ("jiffies:ms ratio %d:%d => CONFIG_HZ=%d\n",
    count_jiffies, count_ms, hz)
  exit ()
}
```

This example script computes the CONFIG_HZ setting of the kernel by using timers that count jiffies and milliseconds, then computing accordingly. (A jiffy is the duration of one tick of the system timer interrupt. It is not an absolute time interval unit, since its duration depends on the clock interrupt frequency of the particular hardware platform). With the `global` statement it is possible to use the variables `count_jiffies` and `count_ms` also in the probe `timer.ms(12345)`. With `++` the value of a variable is incremented by `1`.

4.3.3.2.2   Conditional Statements

There are a number of conditional statements that you can use in SystemTap scripts. The following are probably most common:

If/Else Statements

They are expressed in the following format:

```
if (condition) ➊ statement1 ➋
else ➌ statement2 ➍
```

The `if` statement compares an integer-valued expression to zero. If the condition expression ➊ is non-zero, the first statement ➋ is executed. If the condition expression is zero, the second statement ➍ is executed. The else clause (➌ and ➍) is optional. Both ➋ and ➍ can also be statement blocks.

While Loops

They are expressed in the following format:

```
while (condition) ➊ statement ➋
```

As long as `condition` is non-zero, the statement ➋ is executed. ➋ can also be a statement block. It must change a value so `condition` will eventually be zero.

For Loops

They are a shortcut for `while` loops and are expressed in the following format:

```
for (initialization ➊; conditional ➋; increment ➌) statement
```

The expression specified in ➊ is used to initialize a counter for the number of loop iterations and is executed before execution of the loop starts. The execution of the loop continues until the loop condition ➋ is false. (This expression is checked at the beginning of each loop iteration). The expression specified in ➌ is used to increment the loop counter. It is executed at the end of each loop iteration.

Conditional Operators

The following operators can be used in conditional statements:

==: Is equal to

!=: Is not equal to

>=: Is greater than or equal to

<=: Is less than or equal to

4.4 Example Script

If you have installed the `systemtap-docs` package, you can find a number of useful SystemTap example scripts in `/usr/share/doc/packages/systemtap/examples`.

This section describes a rather simple example script in more detail: `/usr/share/doc/packages/systemtap/examples/network/tcp_connections.stp`.

EXAMPLE 4.5: MONITORING INCOMING TCP CONNECTIONS WITH `tcp_connections.stp`

```
#! /usr/bin/env stap

probe begin {
  printf("%6s %16s %6s %6s %16s\n",
        "UID", "CMD", "PID", "PORT", "IP_SOURCE")
}

probe kernel.function("tcp_accept").return?,
      kernel.function("inet_csk_accept").return? {
  sock = $return
  if (sock != 0)
    printf("%6d %16s %6d %6d %16s\n", uid(), execname(), pid(),
```

```
        inet_get_local_port(sock), inet_get_ip_source(sock))
}
```

This SystemTap script monitors the incoming TCP connections and helps to identify unauthorized or unwanted network access requests in real time. It shows the following information for each new incoming TCP connection accepted by the computer:

- User ID (`UID`)

- Command accepting the connection (`CMD`)

- Process ID of the command (`PID`)

- Port used by the connection (`PORT`)

- IP address from which the TCP connection originated (`IP_SOUCE`)

To run the script, execute

```
stap /usr/share/doc/packages/systemtap/examples/network/tcp_connections.stp
```

and follow the output on the screen. To manually stop the script, press `Ctrl`-`C`.

4.5 User-Space Probing

For debugging user-space applications (like DTrace can do), SUSE Linux Enterprise Server 12 SP1 supports user-space probing with SystemTap: Custom probe points can be inserted in any user-space application. Thus, SystemTap lets you use both Kernel- and user-space probes to debug the behavior of the whole system.

To get the required utrace infrastructure and the uprobes Kernel module for user-space probing, you need to install the `kernel-trace` package in addition to the packages listed in *Section 4.2, "Installation and Setup"*.

utrace implements a framework for controlling user-space tasks. It provides an interface that can be used by various tracing "engines", implemented as loadable Kernel modules. The engines register callback functions for specific events, then attach to whichever thread they want to trace. As the callbacks are made from "safe" places in the Kernel, this allows for great leeway in the kinds of processing the functions can do. Various events can be watched via utrace, for example, system call entry and exit, fork(), signals being sent to the task, etc. More details about the utrace infrastructure are available at http://sourceware.org/systemtap/wiki/utrace.

SystemTap includes support for probing the entry into and return from a function in user-space processes, probing predefined markers in user-space code, and monitoring user-process events.

To check if the currently running Kernel provides the needed utrace support, use the following command:

```
grep CONFIG_UTRACE /boot/config-`uname -r`
```

For more details about user-space probing, refer to https://sourceware.org/system-tap/SystemTap_Beginners_Guide/userspace-probing.html.

4.6 For More Information

This chapter only provides a short SystemTap overview. Refer to the following links for more information about SystemTap:

http://sourceware.org/systemtap/

> SystemTap project home page.

http://sourceware.org/systemtap/wiki/

> Huge collection of useful information about SystemTap, ranging from detailed user and developer documentation to reviews and comparisons with other tools, or Frequently Asked Questions and tips. Also contains collections of SystemTap scripts, examples and usage stories and lists recent talks and papers about SystemTap.

http://sourceware.org/systemtap/documentation.html

> Features a *SystemTap Tutorial*, a *SystemTap Beginner's Guide*, a *Tapset Developer's Guide*, and a *SystemTap Language Reference* in PDF and HTML format. Also lists the relevant man pages.

You can also find the SystemTap language reference and SystemTap tutorial in your installed system under `/usr/share/doc/packages/systemtap`. Example SystemTap scripts are available from the `example` subdirectory.

5 Kernel Probes

Kernel probes are a set of tools to collect Linux kernel debugging and performance information. Developers and system administrators usually use them either to debug the kernel, or to find system performance bottlenecks. The reported data can then be used to tune the system for better performance.

You can insert these probes into any kernel routine, and specify a handler to be invoked after a particular break-point is hit. The main advantage of kernel probes is that you no longer need to rebuild the kernel and reboot the system after you make changes in a probe.

To use kernel probes, you typically need to write or obtain a specific kernel module. Such modules include both the *init* and the *exit* function. The init function (such as `register_kprobe()`) registers one or more probes, while the exit function unregisters them. The registration function defines *where* the probe will be inserted and *which handler* will be called after the probe is hit. To register or unregister a group of probes at one time, you can use relevant `register_<probe_type>probes()` or `unregister_<probe_type>probes()` functions.

Debugging and status messages are typically reported with the `printk` kernel routine. `printk` is a kernel-space equivalent of a user-space `printf` routine. For more information on `printk`, see Logging kernel messages [http://www.win.tue.nl/~aeb/linux/lk/lk-2.html#ss2.8]. Normally, you can view these messages by inspecting the output of the `systemd` journal (see *Book "Administration Guide", Chapter 10 "**journalctl**: Query the* systemd *Journal"*). For more information on log files, see *Chapter 3, Analyzing and Managing System Log Files*.

5.1 Supported Architectures

Kernel probes are *fully* implemented on the following architectures:

- i386

- x86_64 (AMD-64, EM64T)

- ppc64

- arm

- ppc

Kernel probes are *partially* implemented on the following architectures:

- ia64 (does not support probes on instruction `slot1`)

- sparc64 (return probes not yet implemented)

5.2 Types of Kernel Probes

There are three types of kernel probes: *Kprobes, Jprobes,* and *Kretprobes*. Kretprobes are sometimes called *return probes*. You can find source code examples of all three type of probes in the Linux kernel. See the directory `/usr/src/linux/samples/kprobes/` (package `kernel-source`).

5.2.1 Kprobes

Kprobes can be attached to any instruction in the Linux kernel. When Kprobes is registered, it inserts a break-point at the first byte of the probed instruction. When the processor hits this break-point, the processor registers are saved, and the processing passes to Kprobes. First, a *pre-handler* is executed, then the probed instruction is stepped, and, finally a *post-handler* is executed. The control is then passed to the instruction following the probe point.

5.2.2 Jprobes

Jprobes is implemented through the Kprobes mechanism. It is inserted on a function's entry point and allows direct access to the arguments of the function which is being probed. Its handler routine must have the same argument list and return value as the probed function. To end it, call the `jprobe_return()` function.

When a jprobe is hit, the processor registers are saved, and the instruction pointer is directed to the jprobe handler routine. The control then passes to the handler with the same register contents as the function being probed. Finally, the handler calls the `jprobe_return()` function, and switches the control back to the control function.

In general, you can insert multiple probes on one function. Jprobe is, however, limited to only one instance per function.

5.2.3 Return Probe

Return probes are also implemented through Kprobes. When the `register_kretprobe()` function is called, a kprobe is attached to the entry of the probed function. After hitting the probe, the Kernel probes mechanism saves the probed function return address and calls a user-defined return handler. The control is then passed back to the probed function.

Before you call `register_kretprobe()`, you need to set a `maxactive` argument, which specifies how many instances of the function can be probed at the same time. If set too low, you will miss a certain number of probes.

5.3 Kprobes API

The programming interface of Kprobes consists of functions which are used to register and unregister all used kernel probes, and associated probe handlers. For a more detailed description of these functions and their arguments, see the information sources in *Section 5.5, "For More Information"*.

`register_kprobe()`
> Inserts a break-point on a specified address. When the break-point is hit, the `pre_handler` and `post_handler` are called.

`register_jprobe()`
> Inserts a break-point in the specified address. The address needs to be the address of the first instruction of the probed function. When the break-point is hit, the specified handler is run. The handler should have the same argument list and return type as the probed.

`register_kretprobe()`
> Inserts a return probe for the specified function. When the probed function returns, a specified handler is run. This function returns 0 on success, or a negative error number on failure.

`unregister_kprobe()`, `unregister_jprobe()`, `unregister_kretprobe()`
> Removes the specified probe. You can use it any time after the probe has been registered.

`register_kprobes()`, `register_jprobes()`, `register_kretprobes()`
> Inserts each of the probes in the specified array.

`unregister_kprobes()`, `unregister_jprobes()`, `unregister_kretprobes()`
> Removes each of the probes in the specified array.

```
disable_kprobe(), disable_jprobe(), disable_kretprobe()
```
Disables the specified probe temporarily.

```
enable_kprobe(), enable_jprobe(), enable_kretprobe()
```
Temporarily enables disabled probes.

5.4   debugfs Interface

In recent Linux kernels, the Kprobes instrumentation uses the kernel's `debugfs` interface. It can list all registered probes and globally switch all probes on or off.

5.4.1   Listing Registered Kernel Probes

The list of all currently registered probes is in the `/sys/kernel/debug/kprobes/list` file.

```
saturn.example.com:~ # cat /sys/kernel/debug/kprobes/list
c015d71a   k   vfs_read+0x0      [DISABLED]
c011a316   j   do_fork+0x0
c03dedc5   r   tcp_v4_rcv+0x0
```

The first column lists the address in the kernel where the probe is inserted. The second column prints the type of the probe: `k` for kprobe, `j` for jprobe, and `r` for return probe. The third column specifies the symbol, offset and optional module name of the probe. The following optional columns include the status information of the probe. If the probe is inserted on a virtual address which is not valid anymore, it is marked with `[GONE]`. If the probe is temporarily disabled, it is marked with `[DISABLED]`.

5.4.2   How to Switch All Kernel Probes On or Off

The `/sys/kernel/debug/kprobes/enabled` file represents a switch with which you can globally and forcibly turn on or off all the registered kernel probes. To turn them off, simply enter

```
echo "0" > /sys/kernel/debug/kprobes/enabled
```

on the command line as `root`. To turn them on again, enter

```
echo "1" > /sys/kernel/debug/kprobes/enabled
```

Note that this way you do not change the status of the probes. If a probe is temporarily disabled, it will not be enabled automatically but will remain in the `[DISABLED]` state after entering the latter command.

5.5 For More Information

To learn more about kernel probes, look at the following sources of information:

* Thorough but more technically oriented information about kernel probes is in `/usr/src/linux/Documentation/kprobes.txt` (package `kenrel-source`).

* Examples of all three types of probes (together with related `Makefile`) are in the `/usr/src/linux/samples/kprobes/` directory (package `kenrel-source`).

* In-depth information about Linux kernel modules and `printk` kernel routine is in The Linux Kernel Module Programming Guide [http://tldp.org/LDP/lkmpg/2.6/html/lkmpg.html]

* Practical but slightly outdated information about the use of kernel probes can be found in Kernel debugging with Kprobes [http://www.ibm.com/developerworks/library/l-kprobes.html]

6 Hardware-Based Performance Monitoring with Perf

Perf is an interface to access the performance monitoring unit (PMU) of a processor and to record and display software events such as page faults. It supports system-wide, per-thread, and KVM virtualization guest monitoring.

You can store resulting information in a report. This report contains information about, for example, instruction pointers or what code a thread was executing.

Perf consists of two parts:

- Code integrated into the Linux kernel that is responsible for instructing the hardware.

- The **perf** userspace utility that allows you to use the kernel code and helps you analyze gathered data.

6.1 Hardware-Based Monitoring

Performance monitoring means collecting information related to how an application or system performs. This information can be obtained either through software-based means or from the CPU or chipset. Perf integrates both of these methods.

Many modern processors contain a performance monitoring unit (PMU). The design and functionality of a PMU is CPU-specific. For example, the number of registers, counters and features supported will vary by CPU implementation.

Each PMU model consists of a set of registers: the performance monitor configuration (PMC) and the performance monitor data (PMD). Both can be read, but only PMCs are writable. These registers store configuration information and data.

6.2 Sampling and Counting

Perf supports several profiling modes:

- **Counting.** Count the number of occurrences of an event.

- **Event-Based Sampling.** A less exact way of counting: A sample is recorded whenever a certain threshold number of events has occurred.

- **Time-Based Sampling.** A less exact way of counting: A sample is recorded in a defined frequency.

- **Instruction-Based Sampling (AMD64 only).** The processor follows instructions appearing in a given interval and samples which events they produce. This allows following up on individual instructions and seeing which of them is critical to performance.

- **Instruction-Based Sampling (AMD64 only).** The processor follows instructions appearing in a given interval and samples which events they produce. This allows following up on individual instructions and seeing which of them is critical to performance.

6.3   Installing Perf

The Perf kernel code is already included with the default kernel. To be able to use the userspace utility, install the package `perf`.

6.4   Perf Subcommands

To gather the required information, the **perf** tool has several subcommands. This section gives an overview of the most often used commands.

To see help in the form of a man page for any of the subcommands, use either **perf help** *SUB-COMMAND* or **man perf-** *SUBCOMMAND*.

perf stat

> Start a program and create a statistical overview that is displayed after the program quits. **perf stat** is used to count events.

perf record

> Start a program and create a report with performance counter information. The report is stored as `perf.data` in the current directory. **perf record** is used to sample events.

perf report

> Display a report that was previously created with **perf record**.

perf annotate

> Display a report file and an annotated version of the executed code. If debug symbols are installed, you will also see the source code displayed.

`perf list`

List event types that Perf can report with the current kernel and with your CPU. You can filter event types by category—for example, to see hardware events only, use **`perf list hw`**.

The man page for **`perf_event_open`** has short descriptions for the most important events. For example, to find a description of the event `branch-misses`, search for `BRANCH_MISSES` (note the spelling differences):

```
tux > man perf_event_open | grep -A5 BRANCH_MISSES
```

Sometimes, events may be ambiguous. Note that the lowercase hardware event names are not the name of raw hardware events but instead the name of aliases created by Perf. These aliases map to differently named but similarly defined hardware events on each supported processor.

For example, the `cpu-cycles` event is mapped to the hardware event `UNHALTED_CORE_CYCLES` on Intel processors. On AMD processors, however, it is mapped to hardware event `CPU_CLK_UNHALTED`.

Perf also allows measuring raw events specific to your hardware. To look up their descriptions, see the Architecture Software Developer's Manual of your CPU vendor. The relevant documents for AMD64/Intel 64 processors are linked to in *Section 6.7, "For More Information"*.

`perf top`

Display system activity as it happens.

`perf trace`

This command behaves similarly to **`strace`**. With this subcommand, you can see which system calls are executed by a particular thread or process and which signals it receives.

6.5 Counting Particular Types of Event

To count the number of occurrences of an event, such as those displayed by **`perf list`**, use:

```
root # perf stat -e EVENT -a
```

To count multiple types of events at once, list them separated by commas. For example, to count `cpu-cycles` and `instructions`, use:

```
root # perf stat -e cpu-cycles,instructions -a
```

To stop the session, press `Ctrl`-`C`.

You can also count the number of occurrences of an event within a particular time:

```
root # perf stat -e EVENT -a -- sleep TIME
```

Replace *TIME* by a value in seconds.

6.6 Recording Events Specific to Particular Commands

There are various ways to sample events specific to a particular command:

- To create a report for a newly invoked command, use:

```
root # perf record COMMAND
```

  Then, use the started process normally. When you quit the process, the Perf session will also stop.

- To create a report for the entire system while a newly invoked command is running, use:

```
root # perf record -a COMMAND
```

  Then, use the started process normally. When you quit the process, the Perf session will also stop.

- To create a report for an already running process, use:

```
root # perf record -p PID
```

  Replace *PID* with a process ID. To stop the session, press `Ctrl`-`C`.

Afterwards, you can view the gathered data (`perf.data`) using:

```
tux > perf report
```

This will open a pseudo-graphical interface. To receive help, press `H`. To quit, press `Q`.

If you prefer a graphical interface, try the GTK+ interface of Perf:

```
tux > perf report --gtk
```

However, note that the GTK+ interface is very limited in functionality.

6.7 For More Information

This chapter only provides a short overview. Refer to the following links for more information:

https://perf.wiki.kernel.org/index.php/Main_Page

> The project home page. It also features a tutorial on using **perf**.

http://www.brendangregg.com/perf.html

> Unofficial page with many one-line examples of how to use **perf**.

http://web.eece.maine.edu/~vweaver/projects/perf_events/

> Unofficial page with several resources, mostly relating to the Linux kernel code of Perf and its API. This page includes, for example, a CPU compatibility table and a programming guide.

https://www-ssl.intel.com/content/dam/www/public/us/en/documents/manuals/64-ia-32-architectures-software-developer-vol-3b-part-2-manual.pdf

> The *Intel Architectures Software Developer's Manual, Volume 3B*.

https://support.amd.com/TechDocs/24593.pdf

> The *AMD Architecture Programmer's Manual, Volume 2*.

Chapter 7, OProfile—System-Wide Profiler

> Consult this chapter for other performance optimizations.

7 OProfile—System-Wide Profiler

OProfile is a profiler for dynamic program analysis. It investigates the behavior of a running program and gathers information. This information can be viewed and gives hints for further optimization.

It is not necessary to recompile or use wrapper libraries to use OProfile. Not even a kernel patch is needed. Usually, when profiling an application, a small overhead is expected, depending on the workload and sampling frequency.

7.1 Conceptual Overview

OProfile consists of a kernel driver and a daemon for collecting data. It makes use of the hardware performance counters provided on many processors. OProfile is capable of profiling all code including the kernel, kernel modules, kernel interrupt handlers, system shared libraries, and other applications.

Modern processors support profiling through the hardware by performance counters. Depending on the processor, there can be many counters and each of these can be programmed with an event to count. Each counter has a value which determines how often a sample is taken. The lower the value, the more often it is used.

During the post-processing step, all information is collected and instruction addresses are mapped to a function name.

7.2 Installation and Requirements

To use OProfile, install the `oprofile` package that is included with the SLE SDK. OProfile works on AMD64/Intel 64, z Systems, and POWER processors. To find out how to install software from the SDK, refer to *Book "Deployment Guide", Chapter 9 "Installing Modules, Extensions, and Third Party Add-On Products", Section 9.3 "SUSE Software Development Kit (SDK) 12 SP1"*.

It is useful to install the `*-debuginfo` package for the respective application you want to profile. If you want to profile the Kernel, you need the `debuginfo` package as well.

7.3   Available OProfile Utilities

OProfile contains several utilities to handle the profiling process and its profiled data. The following list is a short summary of programs used in this chapter:

opannotate

> Outputs annotated source or assembly listings mixed with profile information. An annotated report can be used in combination with `addr2line` to identify the source file and line where hotspots potentially exist. See `man addr2line` for more information.

opcontrol

> Controls the profiling sessions (start or stop), dumps profile data, and sets up parameters.

ophelp

> Lists available events with short descriptions.

opimport

> Converts sample database files from a foreign binary format to the native format.

opreport

> Generates reports from profiled data.

7.4   Using OProfile

With OProfile, you can profile both the kernel and applications. When profiling the kernel, tell OProfile where to find the `vmlinuz*` file. Use the `--vmlinux` option and point it to `vmlinuz*` (usually in `/boot`). If you need to profile kernel modules, OProfile does this by default. However, make sure you read http://oprofile.sourceforge.net/doc/kernel-profiling.html.

Applications usually do not need to profile the kernel, therefore you should use the `--no-vmlinux` option to reduce the amount of information.

7.4.1   Creating a Report

Starting the daemon, collecting data, stopping the daemon, and creating a report.

1. Open a shell and log in as `root`.

2. Decide if you want to profile with or without the Linux Kernel:

   a. **Profile With the Linux Kernel.** Execute the following commands, because **opcontrol** can only work with uncompressed images:

   ```
   cp /boot/vmlinux-`uname -r`.gz /tmp
   gunzip /tmp/vmlinux*.gz
   opcontrol --vmlinux=/tmp/vmlinux*
   ```

   b. **Profile Without the Linux Kernel.** Use the following command:

   ```
   opcontrol --no-vmlinux
   ```

   If you want to see which functions call other functions in the output, additionally use the `--callgraph` option and set a maximum *DEPTH*:

   ```
   opcontrol --no-vmlinux --callgraph DEPTH
   ```

3. Start the OProfile daemon:

```
opcontrol --start
Using 2.6+ OProfile kernel interface.
Using log file /var/lib/oprofile/samples/oprofiled.log
Daemon started.
Profiler running.
```

4. Now start the application you want to profile.

5. Stop the OProfile daemon:

```
opcontrol --stop
```

6. Dump the collected data to `/var/lib/oprofile/samples`:

```
opcontrol --dump
```

7. Create a report:

```
opreport
Overflow stats not available
```

```
CPU: CPU with timer interrupt, speed 0 MHz (estimated)
Profiling through timer interrupt
          TIMER:0|
  samples|      %|
------------------
    84877 98.3226 no-vmlinux
...
```

8. Shut down the `oprofile` daemon:

```
opcontrol --shutdown
```

7.4.2 Getting Event Configurations

The general procedure for event configuration is as follows:

1. Use first the events `CPU-CLK_UNHALTED` and `INST_RETIRED` to find optimization oppor-
   tunities.

2. Use specific events to find bottlenecks. To list them, use the command **opcontrol** `--`
   `list-events`.

If you need to profile certain events, first check the available events supported by your processor
with the **ophelp** command (example output generated from Intel Core i5 CPU):

```
ophelp
oprofile: available events for CPU type "Intel Architectural Perfmon"

See Intel 64 and IA-32 Architectures Software Developer's Manual
Volume 3B (Document 253669) Chapter 18 for architectural perfmon events
This is a limited set of fallback events because oprofile does not know your CPU
CPU_CLK_UNHALTED: (counter: all))
        Clock cycles when not halted (min count: 6000)
INST_RETIRED: (counter: all))
        number of instructions retired (min count: 6000)
LLC_MISSES: (counter: all))
```

```
        Last level cache demand requests from this core that missed the LLC (min
 count: 6000)
        Unit masks (default 0x41)
        ----------
        0x41: No unit mask
LLC_REFS: (counter: all))
        Last level cache demand requests from this core (min count: 6000)
        Unit masks (default 0x4f)
        ----------
        0x4f: No unit mask
BR_MISS_PRED_RETIRED: (counter: all))
        number of mispredicted branches retired (precise) (min count: 500)
```

You can get the same output from **opcontrol** `--list-events`.

Specify the performance counter events with the option `--event`. Multiple options are possible. This option needs an event name (from **ophelp**) and a sample rate, for example:

```
opcontrol --event=CPU_CLK_UNHALTED:100000
```

 Warning: Setting Sampling Rates with CPU_CLK_UNHALTED

Setting low sampling rates can seriously impair the system performance while high sample rates can disrupt the system to such a high degree that the data is useless. It is recommended to tune the performance metric for being monitored with and without OProfile and to experimentally determine the minimum sample rate that disrupts the performance the least.

7.5 Using OProfile's GUI

The GUI for OProfile can be started as root with **oprof_start**, see *Figure 7.1, "GUI for OProfile"*. Select your events and change the counter, if necessary. Every green line is added to the list of checked events. Hover the mouse over the line to see a help text in the status line below. Use the *Configuration* tab to set the buffer and CPU size, the verbose option and others. Click *Start* to execute OProfile.

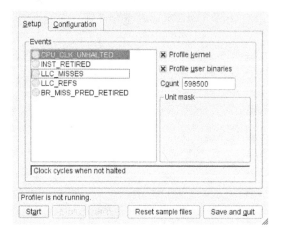

FIGURE 7.1: GUI FOR OPROFILE

7.6 Generating Reports

Before generating a report, make sure OProfile has dumped your data to the `/var/lib/opro-file/samples` directory using the command **opcontrol** `--dump`. A report can be generated with the commands **opreport** or **opannotate**.

Calling **opreport** without any options gives a complete summary. With an executable as an argument, retrieve profile data only from this executable. If you analyze applications written in C++, use the `--demangle smart` option.

The **opannotate** generates output with annotations from source code. Run it with the following options:

```
opannotate --source \
   --base-dirs=BASEDIR \
   --search-dirs= \
   --output-dir=annotated/ \
   /lib/libfoo.so
```

The option `--base-dir` contains a comma separated list of paths which is stripped from debug source files. These paths were searched prior to looking in `--search-dirs`. The `--search-dirs` option is also a comma separated list of directories to search for source files.

Note: Inaccuracies in Annotated Source

Because of compiler optimization, code can disappear and appear in a different place. Use the information in http://oprofile.sourceforge.net/doc/debug-info.html to fully understand its implications.

7.7 For More Information

This chapter only provides a short overview. Refer to the following links for more information:

http://oprofile.sourceforge.net

> The project home page.

Manpages

> Details descriptions about the options of the different tools.

/usr/share/doc/packages/oprofile/oprofile.html

> Contains the OProfile manual.

http://developer.intel.com/

> Architecture reference for Intel processors.

http://www-01.ibm.com/chips/techlib/techlib.nsf/productfamilies/PowerPC/

> Architecture reference for PowerPC64 processors in IBM iSeries, pSeries, and Blade server systems.

IV Resource Management

8 General System Resource Management

Tuning the system is not only about optimizing the kernel or getting the most out of your application, it begins with setting up a lean and fast system. The way you set up your partitions and file systems can influence the server's speed. The number of active services and the way routine tasks are scheduled also affects performance.

8.1 Planning the Installation

A carefully planned installation ensures that the system is set up exactly as you need it for the given purpose. It also saves considerable time when fine tuning the system. All changes suggested in this section can be made in the *Installation Settings* step during the installation. See *Book* "Deployment Guide", *Chapter 6* "Installation with YaST", *Section 6.13* "Installation Settings" for details.

8.1.1 Partitioning

Depending on the server's range of applications and the hardware layout, the partitioning scheme can influence the machine's performance (although to a lesser extent only). It is beyond the scope of this manual to suggest different partitioning schemes for particular workloads. However, the following rules will positively affect performance. They do not apply when using an external storage system.

- Make sure there always is some free space available on the disk, since a full disk delivers inferior performance

- Disperse simultaneous read and write access onto different disks by, for example:

  - using separate disks for the operating system, data, and log files

  - placing a mail server's spool directory on a separate disk

  - distributing the user directories of a home server between different disks

8.1.2   Installation Scope

The installation scope has no direct influence on the machine's performance, but a carefully chosen scope of packages has advantages. It is recommended to install the minimum of packages needed to run the server. A system with a minimum set of packages is easier to maintain and has fewer potential security issues. Furthermore, a tailor made installation scope also ensures that no unnecessary services are started by default.

SUSE Linux Enterprise Server lets you customize the installation scope on the Installation Summary screen. By default, you can select or remove preconfigured patterns for specific tasks, but it is also possible to start the YaST Software Manager for a fine-grained package-based selection.

One or more of the following default patterns may not be needed in all cases:

GNOME Desktop Environment

> Servers rarely need a full desktop environment. In case a graphical environment is needed, a more economical solution such as IceWM can be sufficient.

X Window System

> When solely administrating the server and its applications via command line, consider not installing this pattern. However, keep in mind that it is needed to run GUI applications from a remote machine. If your application is managed by a GUI or if you prefer the GUI version of YaST, keep this pattern.

Print Server

> This pattern is only needed if you want to print from the machine.

8.1.3   Default Target

A running X Window System consumes many resources and is rarely needed on a server. It is strongly recommended to start the system in target `multi-user.target`. You will still be able to remotely start graphical applications.

8.2   Disabling Unnecessary Services

The default installation starts several services (the number varies with the installation scope). Since each service consumes resources, it is recommended to disable the ones not needed. Run *YaST › System › Services Manager* to start the services management module.

If you are using the graphical version of YaST, you can click the column headlines to sort the list of services. Use this to get an overview of which services are currently running. Use the *Start/Stop* button to disable the service for the running session. To permanently disable it, use the *Enable/Disable* button.

The following list shows services that are started by default after the installation of SUSE Linux Enterprise Server. Check which of the components you need, and disable the others:

alsasound

> Loads the Advanced Linux Sound System.

auditd

> A daemon for the Audit system (see *Book* "Security Guide" for details). Disable this if you do not use Audit.

bluez-coldplug

> Handles cold plugging of Bluetooth dongles.

cups

> A printer daemon.

java.binfmt_misc

> Enables the execution of `*.class` or `*.jar` Java programs.

nfs

> Services needed to mount NFS.

smbfs

> Services needed to mount SMB/CIFS file systems from a Windows* server.

splash / splash_early

> Shows the splash screen on start-up.

8.3   File Systems and Disk Access

Hard disks are the slowest components in a computer system and therefore often the cause for a bottleneck. Using the file system that best suits your workload helps to improve performance. Using special mount options or prioritizing a process's I/O priority are further means to speed up the system.

8.3.1 File Systems

SUSE Linux Enterprise Server ships with several different file systems, including BrtFS, Ext3, Ext2, ReiserFS, and XFS. Each file system has its own advantages and disadvantages. Refer to *Book "Storage Administration Guide", Chapter 1 "Overview of File Systems in Linux"* for detailed information.

8.3.1.1 NFS

NFS (Version 3) tuning is covered in detail in the NFS Howto at http://nfs.sourceforge.net/nfs-howto/. The first thing to experiment with when mounting NFS shares is increasing the read write blocksize to `32768` by using the mount options `wsize` and `rsize`.

8.3.2 Disabling Access Time (atime) Updates

Whenever a file is read on a Linux file system, its access time (atime) is updated. As a result, each read-only file access in fact causes a write operation. On a journaling file system two write operations are triggered since the journal will be updated, too. It is recommended to turn this feature off when you do not need to keep track of access times. This can be true for file and Web servers or for network storage.

To turn off access time updates, mount the file system with the `noatime` option. To do so, either edit `/etc/fstab` directly, or use the *Fstab Options* dialog when editing or adding a partition with the YaST Partitioner.

8.3.3 Prioritizing Disk Access with `ionice`

The `ionice` command lets you prioritize disk access for single processes. This enables you to give less I/O priority to background processes with heavy disk access that are not time-critical, such as backup jobs. `ionice` also lets you raise the I/O priority for a specific process to make sure this process always has immediate access to the disk. You can set the following three scheduling classes:

Idle

> A process from the idle scheduling class is only granted disk access when no other process has asked for disk I/O.

Best effort

The default scheduling class used for any process that has not asked for a specific I/O priority. Priority within this class can be adjusted to a level from 0 to 7 (with 0 being the highest priority). Programs running at the same best-effort priority are served in a round-robin fashion. Some kernel versions treat priority within the best-effort class differently—for details, refer to the `ionice(1)` man page.

Real-time

Processes in this class are always granted disk access first. Fine-tune the priority level from 0 to 7 (with 0 being the highest priority). Use with care, since it can starve other processes.

For more details and the exact command syntax refer to the `ionice(1)` man page.

9 Kernel Control Groups

Kernel Control Groups (abbreviated known as "cgroups") are a kernel feature that allows aggregating or partitioning tasks (processes) and all their children into hierarchical organized groups. These hierarchical groups can be configured to show a specialized behavior that helps with tuning the system to make best use of available hardware and network resources.

In the following sections, we often reference kernel documentation such as `/usr/src/linux/Documentation/cgroups/`. These files are part of the `kernel-source` package.

This chapter is just an overview. To use cgroups properly and to avoid performance implications, you must study the provided references.

9.1 Technical Overview and Definitions

The following terms are used in this chapter:

- "cgroup" is another name for Control Groups.

- In a cgroup there is a set of tasks (processes) associated with a set of subsystems that act as parameters constituting an environment for the tasks.

- Subsystems provide the parameters that can be assigned and define CPU sets, freezer, or —more general—"resource controllers" for memory, disk I/O, network traffic, etc.

- cgroups are organized in a tree-structured hierarchy. There can be more than one hierarchy in the system. You use a different or alternate hierarchy to cope with specific situations.

- Every task running in the system is in exactly one of the cgroups in the hierarchy.

9.2 Scenario

See the following resource planning scenario for a better understanding (source: `/usr/src/`
`linux/Documentation/cgroups/cgroups.txt`):

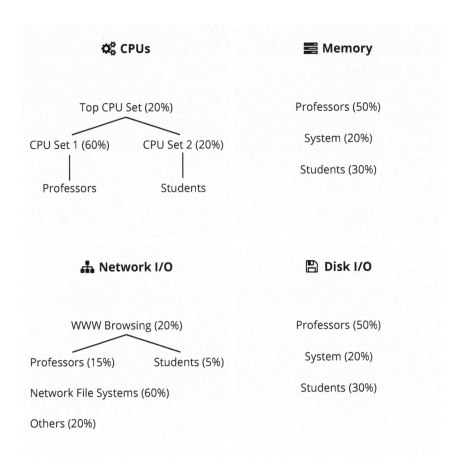

FIGURE 9.1: RESOURCE PLANNING

Web browsers such as Firefox will be part of the Web network class, while the NFS daemons such
as (k)nfsd will be part of the NFS network class. On the other side, Firefox will share appropriate
CPU and memory classes depending on whether a professor or student started it.

9.3 Control Group Subsystems

The following subsystems are available: `cpuset`, `cpu`, `cpuacct`, `memory`, `devices`, `freezer`,
`net_cls`, `net_prio`, `blkio`, `perf_event`, and `hugetlbt`.

Either mount each subsystem separately, for example:

```
mkdir /cpuset /cpu
mount -t cgroup -o cpuset       none /cpuset
mount -t cgroup -o cpu,cpuacct none /cpu
```

or all subsystems in one go; you can use an arbitrary device name (e.g., `none`), which will appear in `/proc/mounts`, for example:

```
mount -t cgroup none /sys/fs/cgroup
```

Some additional information on available subsystems:

`net_cls` **(Identification)**

> The Network classifier cgroup helps with providing identification for controlling processes such as Traffic Controller (tc) or Netfilter (iptables). These controller tools can act on tagged network packets.
>
> For more information, see `/usr/src/linux/Documentation/cgroups/net_cls.txt`.

`net_prio` **(Identification)**

> The Network priority cgroup helps with setting the priority of network packets.
>
> For more information, see `/usr/src/linux/Documentation/cgroups/net_prio.txt`.

`devices` **(Isolation)**

> A system administrator can provide a list of devices that can be accessed by processes under cgroups.
>
> It limits access to a device or a file system on a device to only tasks that belong to the specified cgroup. For more information, see `/usr/src/linux/Documentation/cgroups/devices.txt`.

`freezer` **(Control)**

> The `freezer` subsystem is useful for high-performance computing clusters (HPC clusters). Use it to freeze (stop) all tasks in a group or to stop tasks, if they reach a defined checkpoint. For more information, see `/usr/src/linux/Documentation/cgroups/freezer-subsystem.txt`.
>
> Here are basic commands to use the freezer subsystem:
>
> ```
> mount -t cgroup -o freezer freezer /freezer
> ```

```
# Create a child cgroup:
mkdir /freezer/0
# Put a task into this cgroup:
echo $task_pid > /freezer/0/tasks
# Freeze it:
echo FROZEN > /freezer/0/freezer.state
# Unfreeze (thaw) it:
echo THAWED > /freezer/0/freezer.state
```

perf_event (Control)

perf_event collects performance data.

cpuset (Isolation)

Use cpuset to tie processes to system subsets of CPUs and memory ("memory nodes"). For an example, see *Section 9.4.2, "Example: Cpusets"*.

cpuacct (Accounting)

The CPU accounting controller groups tasks using cgroups and accounts the CPU usage of these groups. For more information, see /usr/src/linux/Documentation/cgroups/ cpuacct.txt.

memory (Resource Control)

- Tracking or limiting memory usage of user space processes.

- Control swap usage by setting swapaccount=1 as a kernel boot parameter.

- Limit LRU (Least Recently Used) pages.

- Anonymous and file cache.

- No limits for kernel memory.

- Maybe in another subsystem if needed.

Note: Protection from Memory Pressure

memory cgroup now offers a mechanism allowing easier workload opt-in isolation. Memory cgroup can define its so called low limit (`memory.low_limit_in_bytes`), which works as a protection from memory pressure. Workloads that need to be isolated from outside memory management activity should set the value to the expected Resident Set Size (RSS) plus some head room. If a memory pressure condition triggers on the system and the particular group is still under its low limit, its memory is protected from reclaim. As a result, workloads outside of the cgroup do not need the aforementioned capping.

For more information, see `/usr/src/linux/Documentation/cgroups/memory.txt`.

`hugetlb` (Resource Control)

The HugeTLB controller accounts the memory allocated in huge pages.

For more information, see `/usr/src/linux/Documentation/cgroups/hugetlb.txt`.

`cpu` (Control)

Share CPU bandwidth between groups with the group scheduling function of CFS (the scheduler). Mechanically complicated.

Blkio (Resource Control)

The Block IO controller is available as a disk I/O controller. With the blkio controller you can currently set policies for proportional bandwidth and for throttling.

These are the basic commands to configure proportional weight division of bandwidth by setting weight values in `blkio.weight`:

```
# Setup in /sys/fs/cgroup
mkdir /sys/fs/cgroup/blkio
mount -t cgroup -o blkio none /sys/fs/cgroup/blkio
# Start two cgroups
mkdir -p /sys/fs/cgroup/blkio/group1 /sys/fs/cgroup/blkio/group2
# Set weights
echo 1000 > /sys/fs/cgroup/blkio/group1/blkio.weight
echo  500 > /sys/fs/cgroup/blkio/group2/blkio.weight
# Write the PIDs of the processes to be controlled to the
# appropriate groups
command1 &
```

Control Group Subsystems

```
echo $! > /sys/fs/cgroup/blkio/group1/tasks


command2 &
echo $! > /sys/fs/cgroup/blkio/group2/tasks
```

These are the basic commands to configure throttling or upper limit policy by setting values in `blkio.throttle.read_bps_device` for reads and `blkio.throttle.write_bps_device` for writes:

```
# Setup in /sys/fs/cgroup
mkdir /sys/fs/cgroup/blkio
mount -t cgroup -o blkio none /sys/fs/cgroup/blkio
# Bandwidth rate of a device for the root group; format:
# <major>:<minor>  <byes_per_second>
echo "8:16  1048576" > /sys/fs/cgroup/blkio/blkio.throttle.read_bps_device
```

For more information about caveats, usage scenarios, and additional parameters, see `/usr/src/linux/Documentation/cgroups/blkio-controller.txt`.

9.4 Using Controller Groups

9.4.1 Prerequisites

To conveniently use cgroups, install the following additional packages:

- `libcgroup-tools` — basic user space tools to simplify resource management

- `libcgroup1` — control groups management library

- `cpuset` — contains the **cset** to manipulate cpusets

- `libcpuset1` — C API to cpusets

- `kernel-source` — only needed for documentation purposes

9.4.2 Example: Cpusets

With the command line proceed as follows:

1. To determine the number of CPUs and memory nodes see `/proc/cpuinfo` and `/proc/zoneinfo`.

2. Create the cpuset hierarchy as a virtual file system (source: `/usr/src/linux/Documentation/cgroups/cpusets.txt`):

```
mount -t cgroup -ocpuset cpuset /sys/fs/cgroup/cpuset
cd /sys/fs/cgroup/cpuset
mkdir Charlie
cd Charlie
# List of CPUs in this cpuset:
echo 2-3 > cpuset.cpus
# List of memory nodes in this cpuset:
echo 1 > cpuset.mems
echo $$ > tasks
# The subshell 'sh' is now running in cpuset Charlie
# The next line should display '/Charlie'
cat /proc/self/cpuset
```

3. Remove the cpuset using shell commands:

```
rmdir /sys/fs/cgroup/cpuset/Charlie
```

This fails as long as this cpuset is in use. First, you must remove the inside cpusets or tasks (processes) that belong to it. Check it with:

```
cat /sys/fs/cgroup/cpuset/Charlie/tasks
```

For background information and additional configuration flags, see `/usr/src/linux/Documentation/cgroups/cpusets.txt`.

With the **cset** tool, proceed as follows:

```
# Determine the number of CPUs and memory nodes
cset set --list
```

```
# Creating the cpuset hierarchy
cset set --cpu=2-3 --mem=1 --set=Charlie
# Starting processes in a cpuset
cset proc --set Charlie --exec -- stress -c 1 &
# Moving existing processes to a cpuset
cset proc --move --pid PID --toset=Charlie
# List task in a cpuset
cset proc --list --set Charlie
# Removing a cpuset
cset set --destroy Charlie
```

9.4.3   Example: cgroups

Using shell commands, proceed as follows:

1. Create the cgroups hierarchy:

```
mount -t cgroup cgroup /sys/fs/cgroup
cd /sys/fs/cgroup/cpuset/cgroup
mkdir priority
cd priority
cat cpu.shares
```

2. Understanding cpu.shares:

   - 1024 is the default (for more information, see /Documentation/scheduler/sched-design-CFS.txt) = 50% usage

   - 1524 = 60% usage

   - 2048 = 67% usage

   - 512 = 40% usage

3. Changing cpu.shares

```
echo 1024 > cpu.shares
```

9.4.4   Setting Directory and File Permissions

This is a simple example. Use the following in `/etc/cgconfig.conf`:

```
group foo {
        perm {
                task {
                        uid = root;
                        gid = users;
                        fperm = 660;
                }
                admin {
                        uid = root;
                        gid = root;
                        fperm = 600;
                        dperm = 750;
                }
        }
}


mount {
        cpu = /mnt/cgroups/cpu;
}
```

Then start the cgconfig service and **stat /mnt/cgroups/cpu/foo/tasks** which should show the permissions mask `660` with `root` as an owner and `users` as a group. **stat /mnt/cgroups/ cpu/foo/** should be `750` and all files (but `tasks`) should have the mask `600`. Note that `fperm` is applied on top of existing file permissions as a mask.

For more information, see the `cgconfig.conf` man page.

9.5   For More Information

- Kernel documentation (package `kernel-source`): files in `/usr/src/linux/Documenta-tion/cgroups`.

- http://lwn.net/Articles/604609/—Brown, Neil: Control Groups Series (2014, 7 parts).

- http://lwn.net/Articles/243795/—Corbet, Jonathan: Controlling memory use in containers (2007).

- http://lwn.net/Articles/236038/—Corbet, Jonathan: Process containers (2007).

10 Automatic Non-Uniform Memory Access (NUMA) Balancing

There are physical limitations to hardware that are encountered when large numbers of CPU and memory are required. For the purposes of this chapter, the important limitation is that there is limited communication bandwidth between the CPUs and the memory. One architecture modification that was introduced to address this is Non-Uniform Memory Access (NUMA).

In this configuration, there are multiple nodes. Each of the nodes contains a subset of all CPUs and memory. The access speed to main memory is determined by the location of the memory relative to the CPU. The performance of a workload depends on the application threads accessing data that is local to the CPU the thread is executing on. Automatic NUMA Balancing is a new feature of SLE 12. Automatic NUMA Balancing migrates data on demand to memory nodes that are local to the CPU accessing that data. Depending on the workload, this can dramatically boost performance when using NUMA hardware.

10.1 Implementation

Automatic NUMA balancing happens in three basic steps:

1. A task scanner periodically scans a portion of a task's address space and marks the memory to force a page fault when the data is next accessed.

2. The next access to the data will result in a NUMA Hinting Fault. Based on this fault, the data can be migrated to a memory node associated with the task accessing the memory.

3. To keep a task, the CPU it is using and the memory it is accessing together, the scheduler groups tasks that share data.

The unmapping of data and page fault handling incurs overhead. However, commonly the overhead will be offset by threads accessing data associated with the CPU.

10.2 Configuration

Static configuration has been the recommended way of tuning workloads on NUMA hardware for some time. To do this, memory policies can be set with **numactl**, **taskset** or **cpusets**. NUMA-aware applications can use special APIs. In cases where the static policies have already been created, automatic NUMA balancing should be disabled as the data access should already be local.

numactl --hardware will show the memory configuration of the machine and whether it supports NUMA or not. This is example output from a 4-node machine.

```
tux > numactl --hardware
available: 4 nodes (0-3)
node 0 cpus: 0 4 8 12 16 20 24 28 32 36 40 44
node 0 size: 16068 MB
node 0 free: 15909 MB
node 1 cpus: 1 5 9 13 17 21 25 29 33 37 41 45
node 1 size: 16157 MB
node 1 free: 15948 MB
node 2 cpus: 2 6 10 14 18 22 26 30 34 38 42 46
node 2 size: 16157 MB
node 2 free: 15981 MB
node 3 cpus: 3 7 11 15 19 23 27 31 35 39 43 47
node 3 size: 16157 MB
node 3 free: 16028 MB
node distances:
node   0   1   2   3
  0:  10  20  20  20
  1:  20  10  20  20
  2:  20  20  10  20
  3:  20  20  20  10
```

Automatic NUMA balancing can be enabled or disabled for the current session by writing NU-MA or NO_NUMA to /sys/kernel/debug/sched_features which will enable or disable the feature respectively. To permanently enable or disable it, use the kernel command line option numa_balancing=[enabled|disabled].

If Automatic NUMA Balancing is enabled, the task scanner behavior can be configured. The task scanner balances the overhead of Automatic NUMA Balancing with the amount of time it takes to identify the best placement of data.

numa_balancing_scan_delay_ms

> The amount of CPU time a thread must consume before its data is scanned. This prevents creating overhead because of short-lived processes.

numa_balancing_scan_period_min_ms **and** numa_balancing_scan_period_max_ms

> Controls how frequently a task's data is scanned. Depending on the locality of the faults the scan rate will increase or decrease. These settings control the min and max scan rates.

numa_balancing_scan_size_mb

> Controls how much address space is scanned when the task scanner is active.

10.3 Monitoring

The most important task is to assign metrics to your workload and measure the performance with Automatic NUMA Balancing enabled and disabled to measure the impact. Profiling tools can be used to monitor local and remote memory accesses if the CPU supports such monitoring. Automatic NUMA Balancing activity can be monitored via the following parameters in /proc/ vmstat:

numa_pte_updates

> The amount of base pages that were marked for NUMA hinting faults.

numa_huge_pte_updates

> The amount of transparent huge pages that were marked for NUMA hinting faults. In combination with numa_pte_updates the total address space that was marked can be calculated.

numa_hint_faults

> Records how many NUMA hinting faults were trapped.

numa_hint_faults_local

> Shows how many of the hinting faults were to local nodes. In combination with numa_hint_faults, the percentage of local versus remote faults can be calculated. A high percentage of local hinting faults indicates that the workload is closer to being converged.

```
numa_pages_migrated
```

Records how many pages were migrated because they were misplaced. As migration is a copying operation, it contributes the largest part of the overhead created by NUMA balancing.

10.4 Impact

The following illustrates a simple test case of a 4-node NUMA machine running the SpecJBB 2005 using a single instance of the JVM with no static tuning around memory policies. Note, however, that the impact for each workload will vary and that this example is based on a pre-release version of SUSE Linux Enterprise Server 12.

```
          Balancing disabled        Balancing enabled
TPut  1     26629.00 (  0.00%)        26507.00 ( -0.46%)
TPut  2     55841.00 (  0.00%)        53592.00 ( -4.03%)
TPut  3     86078.00 (  0.00%)        86443.00 (  0.42%)
TPut  4    116764.00 (  0.00%)       113272.00 ( -2.99%)
TPut  5    143916.00 (  0.00%)       141581.00 ( -1.62%)
TPut  6    166854.00 (  0.00%)       166706.00 ( -0.09%)
TPut  7    195992.00 (  0.00%)       192481.00 ( -1.79%)
TPut  8    222045.00 (  0.00%)       227143.00 (  2.30%)
TPut  9    248872.00 (  0.00%)       250123.00 (  0.50%)
TPut 10    270934.00 (  0.00%)       279314.00 (  3.09%)
TPut 11    297217.00 (  0.00%)       301878.00 (  1.57%)
TPut 12    311021.00 (  0.00%)       326048.00 (  4.83%)
TPut 13    324145.00 (  0.00%)       346855.00 (  7.01%)
TPut 14    345973.00 (  0.00%)       378741.00 (  9.47%)
TPut 15    354199.00 (  0.00%)       394268.00 ( 11.31%)
TPut 16    378016.00 (  0.00%)       426782.00 ( 12.90%)
TPut 17    392553.00 (  0.00%)       437772.00 ( 11.52%)
TPut 18    396630.00 (  0.00%)       456715.00 ( 15.15%)
TPut 19    399114.00 (  0.00%)       484020.00 ( 21.27%)
TPut 20    413907.00 (  0.00%)       493618.00 ( 19.26%)
TPut 21    413173.00 (  0.00%)       510386.00 ( 23.53%)
TPut 22    420256.00 (  0.00%)       521016.00 ( 23.98%)
```

```
TPut 23    425581.00 (  0.00%)    536214.00 ( 26.00%)
TPut 24    429052.00 (  0.00%)    532469.00 ( 24.10%)
TPut 25    426127.00 (  0.00%)    526548.00 ( 23.57%)
TPut 26    422428.00 (  0.00%)    531994.00 ( 25.94%)
TPut 27    424378.00 (  0.00%)    488340.00 ( 15.07%)
TPut 28    419338.00 (  0.00%)    543016.00 ( 29.49%)
TPut 29    403347.00 (  0.00%)    529178.00 ( 31.20%)
TPut 30    408681.00 (  0.00%)    510621.00 ( 24.94%)
TPut 31    406496.00 (  0.00%)    499781.00 ( 22.95%)
TPut 32    404931.00 (  0.00%)    502313.00 ( 24.05%)
TPut 33    397353.00 (  0.00%)    522418.00 ( 31.47%)
TPut 34    382271.00 (  0.00%)    491989.00 ( 28.70%)
TPut 35    388965.00 (  0.00%)    493012.00 ( 26.75%)
TPut 36    374702.00 (  0.00%)    502677.00 ( 34.15%)
TPut 37    367578.00 (  0.00%)    500588.00 ( 36.19%)
TPut 38    367121.00 (  0.00%)    496977.00 ( 35.37%)
TPut 39    355956.00 (  0.00%)    489430.00 ( 37.50%)
TPut 40    350855.00 (  0.00%)    487802.00 ( 39.03%)
TPut 41    345001.00 (  0.00%)    468021.00 ( 35.66%)
TPut 42    336177.00 (  0.00%)    462260.00 ( 37.50%)
TPut 43    329169.00 (  0.00%)    467906.00 ( 42.15%)
TPut 44    329475.00 (  0.00%)    470784.00 ( 42.89%)
TPut 45    323845.00 (  0.00%)    450739.00 ( 39.18%)
TPut 46    323878.00 (  0.00%)    435457.00 ( 34.45%)
TPut 47    310524.00 (  0.00%)    403914.00 ( 30.07%)
TPut 48    311843.00 (  0.00%)    459017.00 ( 47.19%)


                     Balancing Disabled       Balancing Enabled
 Expctd Warehouse          48.00 (  0.00%)          48.00 (  0.00%)
 Expctd Peak Bops     310524.00 (  0.00%)     403914.00 ( 30.07%)
 Actual Warehouse          25.00 (  0.00%)          29.00 ( 16.00%)
 Actual Peak Bops     429052.00 (  0.00%)     543016.00 ( 26.56%)
 SpecJBB Bops            6364.00 (  0.00%)        9368.00 ( 47.20%)
 SpecJBB Bops/JVM        6364.00 (  0.00%)        9368.00 ( 47.20%)
```

Automatic NUMA Balancing takes away some of the pain when tuning workloads for high performance on NUMA machines. Where possible, it is still recommended to statically tune the workload to partition it within each node. However, in all other cases, automatic NUMA balancing should boost performance.

11 Power Management

Power management aims at reducing operating costs for energy and cooling systems while at the same time keeping the performance of a system at a level that matches the current requirements. Thus, power management is always a matter of balancing the actual performance needs and power saving options for a system. Power management can be implemented and used at different levels of the system. A set of specifications for power management functions of devices and the operating system interface to them has been defined in the Advanced Configuration and Power Interface (ACPI). As power savings in server environments can primarily be achieved at the processor level, this chapter introduces some main concepts and highlights some tools for analyzing and influencing relevant parameters.

11.1 Power Management at CPU Level

At the CPU level, you can control power usage in various ways. For example by using idling power states (C-states), changing CPU frequency (P-states), and throttling the CPU (T-states). The following sections give a short introduction to each approach and its significance for power savings. Detailed specifications can be found at http://www.acpi.info/spec.htm.

11.1.1 C-States (Processor Operating States)

Modern processors have several power saving modes called `C-states`. They reflect the capability of an idle processor to turn off unused components in order to save power.

When a processor is in the `C0` state, it is executing instructions. A processor running in any other C-state is idle. The higher the C number, the deeper the CPU sleep mode: more components are shut down to save power. Deeper sleep states can save large amounts of energy. Their downside is that they introduce latency. This means, it takes more time for the CPU to go back to `C0`. Depending on workload (threads waking up, triggering CPU usage and then going back to sleep again for a short period of time) and hardware (for example, interrupt activity of a network device), disabling the deepest sleep states can significantly increase overall performance. For details on how to do so, refer to *Section 11.3.2, "Viewing Kernel Idle Statistics with* **cpupower**".

Some states also have submodes with different power saving latency levels. Which C-states and submodes are supported depends on the respective processor. However, `C1` is always available. *Table 11.1, "C-States"* gives an overview of the most common C-states.

Mode	Definition
C0	Operational state. CPU fully turned on.
C1	First idle state. Stops CPU main internal clocks via software. Bus interface unit and APIC are kept running at full speed.
C2	Stops CPU main internal clocks via hardware. State in which the processor maintains all software-visible states, but may take longer to wake up through interrupts.
C3	Stops all CPU internal clocks. The processor does not need to keep its cache coherent, but maintains other states. Some processors have variations of the C3 state that differ in how long it takes to wake the processor through interrupts.

To avoid needless power consumption, it is recommended to test your workloads with deep sleep states enabled versus deep sleep states disabled. For more information, refer to *Section 11.3.2, "Viewing Kernel Idle Statistics with* `cpupower`*"* or the **`cpupower-idle-set(1)`** man page.

11.1.2   P-States (Processor Performance States)

While a processor operates (in C0 state), it can be in one of several CPU performance states (`P-states`). Whereas C-states are idle states (all but C0), `P-states` are operational states that relate to CPU frequency and voltage.

The higher the P-state, the lower the frequency and voltage at which the processor runs. The number of P-states is processor-specific and the implementation differs across the various types. However, `P0` is always the highest-performance state (except for *Section 11.1.3, "Turbo Features"*). Higher P-state numbers represent slower processor speeds and lower power consumption. For example, a processor in `P3` state runs more slowly and uses less power than a processor running in the `P1` state. To operate at any P-state, the processor must be in the `C0` state, which means that it is working and not idling. The CPU P-states are also defined in the ACPI specification, see http://www.acpi.info/spec.htm.

C-states and P-states can vary independently of one another.

11.1.3 Turbo Features

Turbo features allow to dynamically `overtick` active CPU cores while other cores are in deep sleep states. This increases the performance of active threads while still complying with Thermal Design Power (TDP) limits.

However, the conditions under which a CPU core can use turbo frequencies are architecture-specific. Learn how to evaluate the efficiency of those new features in *Section 11.3, "The* `cpupower` *Tools"*.

11.2 In-Kernel Governors

The in-kernel governors belong to the Linux kernel CPUfreq infrastructure and can be used to dynamically scale processor frequencies at runtime. You can think of the governors as a sort of preconfigured power scheme for the CPU. The CPUfreq governors use P-states to change frequencies and lower power consumption. The dynamic governors can switch between CPU frequencies, based on CPU usage, to allow for power savings while not sacrificing performance.

The following governors are available with the CPUfreq subsystem:

Performance Governor

The CPU frequency is statically set to the highest possible for maximum performance. Consequently, saving power is not the focus of this governor.

See also *Section 11.4.1, "Tuning Options for P-States"*.

Powersave Governor

The CPU frequency is statically set to the lowest possible. This can have severe impact on the performance, as the system will never rise above this frequency no matter how busy the processors are.

However, using this governor often does not lead to the expected power savings as the highest savings can usually be achieved at idle through entering C-states. With the powersave governor, processes run at the lowest frequency and thus take longer to finish. This means it takes longer until the system can go into an idle C-state.

Tuning options: The range of minimum frequencies available to the governor can be adjusted (for example, with the **cpupower** command line tool).

On-demand Governor

The kernel implementation of a dynamic CPU frequency policy: The governor monitors the processor usage. As soon as it exceeds a certain threshold, the governor will set the frequency to the highest available. If the usage is less than the threshold, the next lowest frequency is used. If the system continues to be underemployed, the frequency is again reduced until the lowest available frequency is set.

Important: Drivers and In-kernel Governors

Not all drivers use the in-kernel governors to dynamically scale power frequency at runtime. For example, the `intel_pstate` driver adjusts power frequency itself. Use the **cpupower frequency-info** command to find out which driver your system uses.

11.3 The cpupower Tools

The **cpupower** tools are designed to give an overview of *all* CPU power-related parameters that are supported on a given machine, including turbo (or boost) states. Use the tool set to view and modify settings of the kernel-related CPUfreq and cpuidle systems as well as other settings not related to frequency scaling or idle states. The integrated monitoring framework can access both, kernel-related parameters and hardware statistics, and is thus ideally suited for performance benchmarks. It also helps you to identify the dependencies between turbo and idle states.

After installing the `cpupower` package, view the available **cpupower** subcommands with **cpupower --help**. Access the general man page with **man cpupower**, and the man pages of the subcommands with **man cpupower-***subcommand*.

11.3.1 Viewing Current Settings with `cpupower`

The `cpupower frequency-info` command shows the statistics of the cpufreq driver used in the Kernel. Additionally, it shows if turbo (boost) states are supported and enabled in the BIOS. Run without any options, it shows an output similar to the following:

EXAMPLE 11.1: EXAMPLE OUTPUT OF `cpupower frequency-info`

```
root # cpupower frequency-info
analyzing CPU 0:
  driver: intel_pstate
  CPUs which run at the same hardware frequency: 0
  CPUs which need to have their frequency coordinated by software: 0
  maximum transition latency: 0.97 ms.
  hardware limits: 1.20 GHz - 3.80 GHz
  available cpufreq governors: performance, powersave
  current policy: frequency should be within 1.20 GHz and 3.80 GHz.
                  The governor "powersave" may decide which speed to use
                  within this range.
  current CPU frequency is 3.40 GHz (asserted by call to hardware).
  boost state support:
    Supported: yes
    Active: yes
    3500 MHz max turbo 4 active cores
    3600 MHz max turbo 3 active cores
    3600 MHz max turbo 2 active cores
    3800 MHz max turbo 1 active cores
```

To get the current values for all CPUs, use `cpupower -c all frequency-info`.

11.3.2 Viewing Kernel Idle Statistics with `cpupower`

The `idle-info` subcommand shows the statistics of the cpuidle driver used in the Kernel. It works on all architectures that use the cpuidle Kernel framework.

EXAMPLE 11.2: EXAMPLE OUTPUT OF `cpupower idle-info`

```
root # cpupower idle-info
CPUidle driver: intel_idle
```

```
CPUidle governor: menu

Analyzing CPU 0:
Number of idle states: 6
Available idle states: POLL C1-SNB C1E-SNB C3-SNB C6-SNB C7-SNB
POLL:
Flags/Description: CPUIDLE CORE POLL IDLE
Latency: 0
Usage: 163128
Duration: 17585669
C1-SNB:
Flags/Description: MWAIT 0x00
Latency: 2
Usage: 16170005
Duration: 697658910
C1E-SNB:
Flags/Description: MWAIT 0x01
Latency: 10
Usage: 4421617
Duration: 757797385
C3-SNB:
Flags/Description: MWAIT 0x10
Latency: 80
Usage: 2135929
Duration: 735042875
C6-SNB:
Flags/Description: MWAIT 0x20
Latency: 104
Usage: 53268
Duration: 229366052
C7-SNB:
Flags/Description: MWAIT 0x30
Latency: 109
Usage: 62593595
Duration: 324631233978
```

After finding out which processor idle states are supported with **cpupower idle-info**, individual states can be disabled using the **cpupower idle-set** command. Typically one wants to disable the deepest sleep state, for example:

```
cpupower idle-set -d 5
```

Or, for disabling all CPUs with latencies equal to or higher than 80:

```
cpupower idle-set -D 80
```

11.3.3   Monitoring Kernel and Hardware Statistics with cpupower

Use the **monitor** subcommand to report processor topology, and monitor frequency and idle power state statistics over a certain period of time. The default interval is 1 second, but it can be changed with the -i. Independent processor sleep states and frequency counters are implemented in the tool—some retrieved from kernel statistics, others reading out hardware registers. The available monitors depend on the underlying hardware and the system. List them with **cpupower monitor -l**. For a description of the individual monitors, refer to the cpupower-monitor man page.

The **monitor** subcommand allows you to execute performance benchmarks. To compare Kernel statistics with hardware statistics for specific workloads, concatenate the respective command, for example:

```
cpupower monitor db_test.sh
```

EXAMPLE 11.3: EXAMPLE cpupower monitor OUTPUT

```
root # cpupower monitor
|Mperf                    || Idle_Stats
 ❶                           ❷
CPU | C0   | Cx   | Freq || POLL | C1    | C2    | C3
   0|  3.71| 96.29| 2833||  0.00|  0.00|  0.02| 96.32
   1| 100.0| -0.00| 2833||  0.00|  0.00|  0.00|  0.00
   2|  9.06| 90.94| 1983||  0.00|  7.69|  6.98| 76.45
   3|  7.43| 92.57| 2039||  0.00|  2.60| 12.62| 77.52
```

1 Mperf shows the average frequency of a CPU, including boost frequencies, over a period of time. Additionally, it shows the percentage of time the CPU has been active (`C0`) or in any sleep state (`Cx`). As the turbo states are managed by the BIOS, it is impossible to get the frequency values at a given instant. On modern processors with turbo features the Mperf monitor is the only way to find out about the frequency a certain CPU has been running in.

2 Idle_Stats shows the statistics of the cpuidle kernel subsystem. The kernel updates these values every time an idle state is entered or left. Therefore there can be some inaccuracy when cores are in an idle state for some time when the measure starts or ends.

Apart from the (general) monitors in the example above, other architecture-specific monitors are available. For detailed information, refer to the **cpupower-monitor** man page.

By comparing the values of the individual monitors, you can find correlations and dependencies and evaluate how well the power saving mechanism works for a certain workload. In *Example 11.3* you can see that CPU `0` is idle (the value of `Cx` is near 100%), but runs at a very high frequency. This is because the CPUs `0` and `1` have the same frequency values which means that there is a dependency between them.

11.3.4   Modifying Current Settings with **cpupower**

You can use **cpupower frequency-set** command as `root` to modify current settings. It allows you to set values for the minimum or maximum CPU frequency the governor may select or to create a new governor. With the `-c` option, you can also specify for which of the processors the settings should be modified. That makes it easy to use a consistent policy across all processors without adjusting the settings for each processor individually. For more details and the available options, refer to the **cpupower-freqency-set** man page or run **cpupower frequency-set** `--help`.

11.4   Special Tuning Options

The following sections highlight some of the most relevant settings that you might want to touch.

11.4.1 Tuning Options for P-States

The CPUfreq subsystem offers several tuning options for P-states: You can switch between the different governors, influence minimum or maximum CPU frequency to be used or change individual governor parameters.

To switch to another governor at runtime, use **cpupower frequency-set** with the -g option. For example, running the following command (as root) will activate the performance governor:

```
cpupower frequency-set -g performance
```

To set values for the minimum or maximum CPU frequency the governor may select, use the -d or -u option, respectively.

11.5 Troubleshooting

BIOS options enabled?

   To use C-states or P-states, check your BIOS options:

   - To use C-states, make sure to enable CPU C State or similar options to benefit from power savings at idle.

   - To use P-states and the CPUfreq governors, make sure to enable Processor Performance States options or similar.

   In case of a CPU upgrade, make sure to upgrade your BIOS, too. The BIOS needs to know the new CPU and its frequency stepping to pass this information on to the operating system.

Log file information?

   Check the systemd journal (see *Book "Administration Guide", Chapter 10 "***journalctl***: Query the* systemd *Journal"*) for any output regarding the CPUfreq subsystem. Only severe errors are reported there.

   If you suspect problems with the CPUfreq subsystem on your machine, you can also enable additional debug output. To do so, either use **cpufreq.debug=7** as boot parameter or execute the following command as root:

```
echo 7 > /sys/module/cpufreq/parameters/debug
```

This will cause CPUfreq to log more information to **dmesg** on state transitions, which is useful for diagnosis. But as this additional output of kernel messages can be rather comprehensive, use it only if you are fairly sure that a problem exists.

11.6   For More Information

Platforms with a Baseboard Management Controller (BMC) may have additional power management configuration options accessible via the service processor. These configurations are vendor specific and therefore not subject of this guide. For more information, refer to the manuals provided by your vendor. For example, *HP ProLiant Server Power Management on SUSE Linux Enterprise Server 11—Integration Note* provides detailed information how the HP platform specific power management features interact with the Linux Kernel. The paper is available from http://h18004.www1.hp.com/products/servers/technology/whitepapers/os-techwp.html.

V Kernel Tuning

12 Tuning I/O Performance

I/O scheduling controls how input/output operations will be submitted to storage. SUSE Linux Enterprise Server offers various I/O algorithms—called `elevators`— suiting different workloads. Elevators can help to reduce seek operations, can prioritize I/O requests, or make sure, and I/O request is carried out before a given deadline.

Choosing the best suited I/O elevator not only depends on the workload, but on the hardware, too. Single ATA disk systems, SSDs, RAID arrays, or network storage systems, for example, each require different tuning strategies.

12.1 Switching I/O Scheduling

SUSE Linux Enterprise Server lets you set a default I/O scheduler at boot-time, which can be changed on the fly per block device. This makes it possible to set different algorithms, for example, for the device hosting the system partition and the device hosting a database.

By default the `CFQ` (Completely Fair Queuing) scheduler is used. To change this default, use the following boot parameter:

```
elevator=SCHEDULER
```

Replace *SCHEDULER* with one of the values `cfq`, `noop`, or `deadline`. See *Section 12.2, "Available I/O Elevators"* for details.

To change the elevator for a specific device in the running system, run the following command:

```
echo SCHEDULER > /sys/block/DEVICE/queue/scheduler
```

Here, *SCHEDULER* is one of `cfq`, `noop`, or `deadline`. *DEVICE* is the block device (`sda` for example).

 Note: Default Scheduler on IBM z Systems

On IBM z Systems, the default I/O scheduler for a storage device is set by the device driver.

12.2 Available I/O Elevators

In the following elevators available on SUSE Linux Enterprise Server are listed. Each elevator has a set of tunable parameters, which can be set with the following command:

```
echo VALUE > /sys/block/DEVICE/queue/iosched/TUNABLE
```

where *VALUE* is the desired value for the *TUNABLE* and *DEVICE* the block device.

To find out which elevator is the current default, run the following command. The currently selected scheduler is listed in brackets:

```
jupiter:~ # cat /sys/block/sda/queue/scheduler
noop deadline [cfq]
```

12.2.1 CFQ (Completely Fair Queuing)

CFQ is a fairness-oriented scheduler and is used by default on SUSE Linux Enterprise Server. The algorithm assigns each thread a time slice in which it is allowed to submit I/O to disk. This way each thread gets a fair share of I/O throughput. It also allows assigning tasks I/O priorities which are taken into account during scheduling decisions (see **man 1 ionice**). The CFQ scheduler has the following tunable parameters:

/sys/block/*DEVICE*/queue/iosched/slice_idle

> When a task has no more I/O to submit in its time slice, the I/O scheduler waits for a while before scheduling the next thread to improve locality of I/O. Additionally, the I/O scheduler avoids starving processes doing dependent I/O. A process does dependent I/O if it needs a result of one I/O in order to submit another I/O. For example, if you first need to read an index block in order to find out a data block to read, these two reads form a dependent I/O.
>
> For media where locality does not play a big role (SSDs, SANs with lots of disks) setting /sys/block/<*device*>/queue/iosched/slice_idle to 0 can improve the throughput considerably.

/sys/block/*DEVICE*/queue/iosched/quantum

> This option limits the maximum number of requests that are being processed at once by the device. The default value is 4. For a storage with several disks, this setting can unnecessarily limit parallel processing of requests. Therefore, increasing the value can improve

performance. However, it can also cause latency of certain I/O operations to increase because more requests are buffered inside the storage. When changing this value, you can also consider tuning `/sys/block/DEVICE/queue/iosched/slice_async_rq` (the default value is `2`). This limits the maximum number of asynchronous requests—usually write requests—that are submitted in one time slice.

`/sys/block/DEVICE/queue/iosched/low_latency`

When enabled (which is the default on SUSE Linux Enterprise Server) the scheduler may dynamically adjust the length of the time slice by aiming to meet a tuning parameter called the `target_latency`. Time slices are recomputed to meet this `target_latency` and ensure that processes get fair access within a bounded length of time.

`/sys/block/DEVICE/queue/iosched/target_latency`

Contains an estimated latency time for the `CFQ`. `CFQ` will use it to calculate the time slice used for every task.

`/sys/block/DEVICE/queue/iosched/group_idle`

To avoid starving of blkio cgroups doing dependent I/O, CFQ waits a bit after completion of I/O for one blkio cgroup before scheduling I/O from a different blkio cgroup. When `slice_idle` is set, this parameter does not have big effect. However, for fast media, the overhead of `slice_idle` is generally undesirable. Disabling `slice_idle` and setting `group_idle` is a method to avoid starvation of blkio cgroups doing dependent I/O with lower overhead.

EXAMPLE 12.1: INCREASING INDIVIDUAL THREAD THROUGHPUT USING CFQ

In SUSE Linux Enterprise Server 12 SP1, the `low_latency` tuning parameter is enabled by default to ensure that processes get fair access within a bounded length of time. (Note that this parameter was not enabled in versions prior to SUSE Linux Enterprise 12.)

This is usually preferred in a server scenario where processes are executing I/O as part of transactions, as it makes the time needed for each transaction predictable. However, there are scenarios where that is not the desired behavior:

- If the performance metric of interest is the peak performance of a single process when there is I/O contention.

- If a workload must complete as quickly as possible and there are multiple sources of I/O. In this case, unfair treatment from the I/O scheduler may allow the transactions to complete faster: Processes take their full slice and exit quickly, resulting in reduced overall contention.

To address this, there are two options—increase `target_latency` or disable `low_latency`. As with all tuning parameters it is important to verify your workload behaves as expected before and after the tuning modification. Take careful note of whether your workload depends on individual process peak performance or scales better with fairness. It should also be noted that the performance will depend on the underlying storage and the correct tuning option for one installation may not be universally true.

Find below an example that does not control when I/O starts but is simple enough to demonstrate the point. 32 processes are writing a small amount of data to disk in parallel. Using the SUSE Linux Enterprise Server default (enabling `low_latency`), the result looks as follows:

```
root # echo 1 > /sys/block/sda/queue/iosched/low_latency
root # time ./dd-test.sh
10485760 bytes (10 MB) copied, 2.62464 s, 4.0 MB/s
10485760 bytes (10 MB) copied, 3.29624 s, 3.2 MB/s
10485760 bytes (10 MB) copied, 3.56341 s, 2.9 MB/s
10485760 bytes (10 MB) copied, 3.56908 s, 2.9 MB/s
10485760 bytes (10 MB) copied, 3.53043 s, 3.0 MB/s
10485760 bytes (10 MB) copied, 3.57511 s, 2.9 MB/s
10485760 bytes (10 MB) copied, 3.53672 s, 3.0 MB/s
10485760 bytes (10 MB) copied, 3.5433 s, 3.0 MB/s
10485760 bytes (10 MB) copied, 3.65474 s, 2.9 MB/s
10485760 bytes (10 MB) copied, 3.63694 s, 2.9 MB/s
10485760 bytes (10 MB) copied, 3.90122 s, 2.7 MB/s
10485760 bytes (10 MB) copied, 3.88507 s, 2.7 MB/s
10485760 bytes (10 MB) copied, 3.86135 s, 2.7 MB/s
10485760 bytes (10 MB) copied, 3.84553 s, 2.7 MB/s
10485760 bytes (10 MB) copied, 3.88871 s, 2.7 MB/s
10485760 bytes (10 MB) copied, 3.94943 s, 2.7 MB/s
10485760 bytes (10 MB) copied, 4.12731 s, 2.5 MB/s
10485760 bytes (10 MB) copied, 4.15106 s, 2.5 MB/s
10485760 bytes (10 MB) copied, 4.21601 s, 2.5 MB/s
10485760 bytes (10 MB) copied, 4.35004 s, 2.4 MB/s
10485760 bytes (10 MB) copied, 4.33387 s, 2.4 MB/s
10485760 bytes (10 MB) copied, 4.55434 s, 2.3 MB/s
10485760 bytes (10 MB) copied, 4.52283 s, 2.3 MB/s
```

```
10485760 bytes (10 MB) copied, 4.52682 s, 2.3 MB/s
10485760 bytes (10 MB) copied, 4.56176 s, 2.3 MB/s
10485760 bytes (10 MB) copied, 4.62727 s, 2.3 MB/s
10485760 bytes (10 MB) copied, 4.78958 s, 2.2 MB/s
10485760 bytes (10 MB) copied, 4.79772 s, 2.2 MB/s
10485760 bytes (10 MB) copied, 4.78004 s, 2.2 MB/s
10485760 bytes (10 MB) copied, 4.77994 s, 2.2 MB/s
10485760 bytes (10 MB) copied, 4.86114 s, 2.2 MB/s
10485760 bytes (10 MB) copied, 4.88062 s, 2.1 MB/s


real    0m4.978s
user    0m0.112s
sys     0m1.544s
```

Note that each process completes in similar times. This is the `CFQ` scheduler meeting its `target_latency`: Each process has fair access to storage.

Note that the earlier processes complete somewhat faster. This happens because the start time of the processes is not identical. In a more complicated example, it is possible to control for this.

This is what happens when low_latency is disabled:

```
root # echo 0 > /sys/block/sda/queue/iosched/low_latency
root # time ./dd-test.sh
10485760 bytes (10 MB) copied, 0.813519 s, 12.9 MB/s
10485760 bytes (10 MB) copied, 0.788106 s, 13.3 MB/s
10485760 bytes (10 MB) copied, 0.800404 s, 13.1 MB/s
10485760 bytes (10 MB) copied, 0.816398 s, 12.8 MB/s
10485760 bytes (10 MB) copied, 0.959087 s, 10.9 MB/s
10485760 bytes (10 MB) copied, 1.09563 s, 9.6 MB/s
10485760 bytes (10 MB) copied, 1.18716 s, 8.8 MB/s
10485760 bytes (10 MB) copied, 1.27661 s, 8.2 MB/s
10485760 bytes (10 MB) copied, 1.46312 s, 7.2 MB/s
10485760 bytes (10 MB) copied, 1.55489 s, 6.7 MB/s
10485760 bytes (10 MB) copied, 1.64277 s, 6.4 MB/s
10485760 bytes (10 MB) copied, 1.78196 s, 5.9 MB/s
10485760 bytes (10 MB) copied, 1.87496 s, 5.6 MB/s
```

```
10485760 bytes (10 MB) copied, 1.9461 s, 5.4 MB/s
10485760 bytes (10 MB) copied, 2.08351 s, 5.0 MB/s
10485760 bytes (10 MB) copied, 2.28003 s, 4.6 MB/s
10485760 bytes (10 MB) copied, 2.42979 s, 4.3 MB/s
10485760 bytes (10 MB) copied, 2.54564 s, 4.1 MB/s
10485760 bytes (10 MB) copied, 2.6411 s, 4.0 MB/s
10485760 bytes (10 MB) copied, 2.75171 s, 3.8 MB/s
10485760 bytes (10 MB) copied, 2.86162 s, 3.7 MB/s
10485760 bytes (10 MB) copied, 2.98453 s, 3.5 MB/s
10485760 bytes (10 MB) copied, 3.13723 s, 3.3 MB/s
10485760 bytes (10 MB) copied, 3.36399 s, 3.1 MB/s
10485760 bytes (10 MB) copied, 3.60018 s, 2.9 MB/s
10485760 bytes (10 MB) copied, 3.58151 s, 2.9 MB/s
10485760 bytes (10 MB) copied, 3.67385 s, 2.9 MB/s
10485760 bytes (10 MB) copied, 3.69471 s, 2.8 MB/s
10485760 bytes (10 MB) copied, 3.66658 s, 2.9 MB/s
10485760 bytes (10 MB) copied, 3.81495 s, 2.7 MB/s
10485760 bytes (10 MB) copied, 4.10172 s, 2.6 MB/s
10485760 bytes (10 MB) copied, 4.0966 s, 2.6 MB/s

real    0m3.505s
user    0m0.160s
sys     0m1.516s
```

Note that the time processes take to complete is spread much wider as processes are not getting fair access. Some processes complete faster and exit, allowing the total workload to complete faster, and some processes measure higher apparent I/O performance. It is also important to note that this example may not behave similarly on all systems as the results depend on the resources of the machine and the underlying storage.

It is important to emphasize that neither tuning option is inherently better than the other. Both are best in different circumstances and it is important to understand the requirements of your workload and tune accordingly.

12.2.2 NOOP

A trivial scheduler that only passes down the I/O that comes to it. Useful for checking whether complex I/O scheduling decisions of other schedulers are causing I/O performance regressions.

This scheduler is recommended for setups with devices that do I/O scheduling themselves, such as intelligent storage or in multipathing environments. If you choose a more complicated scheduler on the host, the scheduler of the host and the scheduler of the storage device compete with each other. This can decrease performance. The storage device can usually determine best how to schedule I/O.

For similar reasons, this scheduler is also recommended for use within virtual machines.

The NOOP scheduler can be useful for devices that do not depend on mechanical movement, like SSDs. Usually, the DEADLINE I/O scheduler is a better choice for these devices. However, NOOP creates less overhead and thus can on certain workloads increase performance.

12.2.3 DEADLINE

DEADLINE is a latency-oriented I/O scheduler. Each I/O request is assigned a deadline. Usually, requests are stored in queues (read and write) sorted by sector numbers. The DEADLINE algorithm maintains two additional queues (read and write) in which requests are sorted by deadline. As long as no request has timed out, the "sector" queue is used. When timeouts occur, requests from the "deadline" queue are served until there are no more expired requests. Generally, the algorithm prefers reads over writes.

This scheduler can provide a superior throughput over the CFQ I/O scheduler in cases where several threads read and write and fairness is not an issue. For example, for several parallel readers from a SAN and for databases (especially when using "TCQ" disks). The DEADLINE scheduler has the following tunable parameters:

`/sys/block/<device>/queue/iosched/writes_starved`

> Controls how many reads can be sent to disk before it is possible to send writes. A value of 3 means, that three read operations are carried out for one write operation.

`/sys/block/<device>/queue/iosched/read_expire`

> Sets the deadline (current time plus the read_expire value) for read operations in milliseconds. The default is 500.

`/sys/block/<device>/queue/iosched/write_expire`

> `/sys/block/<device>/queue/iosched/read_expire` Sets the deadline (current time plus the read_expire value) for read operations in milliseconds. The default is 500.

12.3   I/O Barrier Tuning

Most file systems (such as XFS, Ext3, Ext4, or reiserfs) send write barriers to disk after fsync or during transaction commits. Write barriers enforce proper ordering of writes, making volatile disk write caches safe to use (at some performance penalty). If your disks are battery-backed in one way or another, disabling barriers can safely improve performance.

Sending write barriers can be disabled using the `barrier=0` mount option (for Ext3, Ext4, and reiserfs), or using the `nobarrier` mount option (for XFS).

 Warning: Disabling Barriers Can Lead to Data Loss

Disabling barriers when disks cannot guarantee caches are properly written in case of power failure can lead to severe file system corruption and data loss.

13 Tuning the Task Scheduler

Modern operating systems, such as SUSE® Linux Enterprise Server, normally run many different tasks at the same time. For example, you can be searching in a text file while receiving an e-mail and copying a big file to an external hard disk. These simple tasks require many additional processes to be run by the system. To provide each task with its required system resources, the Linux kernel needs a tool to distribute available system resources to individual tasks. And this is exactly what the *task scheduler* does.

The following sections explain the most important terms related to a process scheduling. They also introduce information about the task scheduler policy, scheduling algorithm, description of the task scheduler used by SUSE Linux Enterprise Server, and references to other sources of relevant information.

13.1   Introduction

The Linux kernel controls the way that tasks (or processes) are managed on the system. The task scheduler, sometimes called *process scheduler*, is the part of the kernel that decides which task to run next. It is responsible for best using system resources to guarantee that multiple tasks are being executed simultaneously. This makes it a core component of any multitasking operating system.

13.1.1   Preemption

The theory behind task scheduling is very simple. If there are runnable processes in a system, at least one process must always be running. If there are more runnable processes than processors in a system, not all the processes can be running all the time.

Therefore, some processes need to be stopped temporarily, or *suspended*, so that others can be running again. The scheduler decides what process in the queue will run next.

As already mentioned, Linux, like all other Unix variants, is a *multitasking* operating system. That means that several tasks can be running at the same time. Linux provides a so called *preemptive* multitasking, where the scheduler decides when a process is suspended. This forced suspension is called *preemption*. All Unix flavors have been providing preemptive multitasking since the beginning.

13.1.2   Timeslice

The time period for which a process will be running before it is *preempted* is defined in advance. It is called a *timeslice* of a process and represents the amount of processor time that is provided to each process. By assigning timeslices, the scheduler makes global decisions for the running system, and prevents individual processes from dominating over the processor resources.

13.1.3   Process Priority

The scheduler evaluates processes based on their priority. To calculate the current priority of a process, the task scheduler uses complex algorithms. As a result, each process is given a value according to which it is "allowed" to run on a processor.

13.2   Process Classification

Processes are usually classified according to their purpose and behavior. Although the borderline is not always clearly distinct, generally two criteria are used to sort them. These criteria are independent and do not exclude each other.

One approach is to classify a process either *I/O-bound* or *processor-bound*.

I/O-bound

> I/O stands for Input/Output devices, such as keyboards, mice, or optical and hard disks. *I/O-bound processes* spend the majority of time submitting and waiting for requests. They are run very frequently, but for short time intervals, not to block other processes waiting for I/O requests.

processor-bound

> On the other hand, *processor-bound* tasks use their time to execute a code, and usually run until they are preempted by the scheduler. They do not block processes waiting for I/O requests, and, therefore, can be run less frequently but for longer time intervals.

Another approach is to divide processes by type into *interactive, batch,* and *real-time* processes.

- *Interactive* processes spend a lot of time waiting for I/O requests, such as keyboard or mouse operations. The scheduler must wake up such processes quickly on user request, or the user will find the environment unresponsive. The typical delay is approximately 100 ms. Office applications, text editors or image manipulation programs represent typical interactive processes.

- *Batch* processes often run in the background and do not need to be responsive. They usually receive lower priority from the scheduler. Multimedia converters, database search engines, or log files analyzers are typical examples of batch processes.

- *Real-time* processes must never be blocked by low-priority processes, and the scheduler guarantees a short response time to them. Applications for editing multimedia content are a good example here.

13.3 Completely Fair Scheduler

Since the Linux kernel version 2.6.23, a new approach has been taken to the scheduling of runnable processes. Completely Fair Scheduler (CFS) became the default Linux kernel scheduler. Since then, important changes and improvements have been made. The information in this chapter applies to SUSE Linux Enterprise Server with kernel version 2.6.32 and higher (including 3.x kernels). The scheduler environment was divided into several parts, and three main new features were introduced:

Modular Scheduler Core

The core of the scheduler was enhanced with *scheduling classes*. These classes are modular and represent scheduling policies.

Completely Fair Scheduler

Introduced in kernel 2.6.23 and extended in 2.6.24, CFS tries to assure that each process obtains its "fair" share of the processor time.

Group Scheduling

For example, if you split processes into groups according to which user is running them, CFS tries to provide each of these groups with the same amount of processor time.

As a result, CFS brings optimized scheduling for both servers and desktops.

13.3.1 How CFS Works

CFS tries to guarantee a fair approach to each runnable task. To find the most balanced way of task scheduling, it uses the concept of *red-black tree*. A red-black tree is a type of self-balancing data search tree which provides inserting and removing entries in a reasonable way so that it remains well balanced. For more information, see the wiki pages of Red-black tree [http://en.wikipedia.org/wiki/Red_black_tree].

When a task enters into the *run queue* (a planned time line of processes to be executed next), the scheduler records the current time. While the process waits for processor time, its "wait" value gets incremented by an amount derived from the total number of tasks currently in the run queue and the process priority. As soon as the processor runs the task, its "wait" value gets decremented. If the value drops below a certain level, the task is preempted by the scheduler and other tasks get closer to the processor. By this algorithm, CFS tries to reach the ideal state where the "wait" value is always zero.

13.3.2 Grouping Processes

Since the Linux kernel version 2.6.24, CFS can be tuned to be fair to users or groups rather than to tasks only. Runnable tasks are then grouped to form entities, and CFS tries to be fair to these entities instead of individual runnable tasks. The scheduler also tries to be fair to individual tasks within these entities.

Tasks can be grouped in two mutually exclusive ways:

- By user IDs

- By kernel control groups.

The way the kernel scheduler lets you group the runnable tasks depends on setting the kernel compile-time options `CONFIG_FAIR_USER_SCHED` and `CONFIG_FAIR_CGROUP_SCHED`. The default setting in SUSE® Linux Enterprise Server 12 SP1 is to use control groups, which lets you create groups as needed. For more information, see *Chapter 9, Kernel Control Groups*.

13.3.3   Kernel Configuration Options

Basic aspects of the task scheduler behavior can be set through the kernel configuration options. Setting these options is part of the kernel compilation process. Because kernel compilation process is a complex task and out of this document's scope, refer to relevant source of information.

 Warning: Kernel Compilation

If you run SUSE Linux Enterprise Server on a kernel that was not shipped with it, for example on a self-compiled kernel, you lose the entire support entitlement.

13.3.4   Terminology

Documents regarding task scheduling policy often use several technical terms which you need to know to understand the information correctly. Here are some:

Latency

Delay between the time a process is scheduled to run and the actual process execution.

Granularity

The relation between granularity and latency can be expressed by the following equation:

```
gran = ( lat / rtasks ) - ( lat / rtasks / rtasks )
```

where *gran* stands for granularity, *lat* stand for latency, and *rtasks* is the number of running tasks.

13.3.4.1   Scheduling Policies

The Linux kernel supports the following scheduling policies:

SCHED_FIFO

Scheduling policy designed for special time-critical applications. It uses the First In-First Out scheduling algorithm.

SCHED_BATCH

Scheduling policy designed for CPU-intensive tasks.

SCHED_IDLE

> Scheduling policy intended for *very* low prioritized tasks.

SCHED_OTHER

> Default Linux time-sharing scheduling policy used by the majority of processes.

SCHED_RR

> Similar to `SCHED_FIFO`, but uses the Round Robin scheduling algorithm.

13.3.5   Changing Real-time Attributes of Processes with `chrt`

The **chrt** command sets or retrieves the real-time scheduling attributes of a running process, or runs a command with the specified attributes. You can get or retrieve both the scheduling policy and priority of a process.

In the following examples, a process whose PID is 16244 is used.

To *retrieve* the real-time attributes of an existing task:

```
root # chrt -p 16244
pid 16244's current scheduling policy: SCHED_OTHER
pid 16244's current scheduling priority: 0
```

Before setting a new scheduling policy on the process, you need to find out the minimum and maximum valid priorities for each scheduling algorithm:

```
root # chrt -m
SCHED_OTHER min/max priority : 0/0
SCHED_FIFO min/max priority : 1/99
SCHED_RR min/max priority : 1/99
SCHED_BATCH min/max priority : 0/0
SCHED_IDLE min/max priority : 0/0
```

In the above example, SCHED_OTHER, SCHED_BATCH, SCHED_IDLE polices only allow for priority 0, while that of SCHED_FIFO and SCHED_RR can range from 1 to 99.

To set SCHED_BATCH scheduling policy:

```
root # chrt -b -p 0 16244
pid 16244's current scheduling policy: SCHED_BATCH
```

```
pid 16244's current scheduling priority: 0
```

For more information on **chrt**, see its man page (**man 1 chrt**).

13.3.6   Runtime Tuning with `sysctl`

The **sysctl** interface for examining and changing kernel parameters at runtime introduces important variables by means of which you can change the default behavior of the task scheduler. The syntax of the **sysctl** is simple, and all the following commands must be entered on the command line as `root`.

To read a value from a kernel variable, enter

```
sysctl variable
```

To assign a value, enter

```
sysctl variable=value
```

To get a list of all scheduler related **sysctl** variables, enter

```
sysctl -A | grep "sched" | grep -v"domain"
```

```
root # sysctl -A | grep "sched" | grep -v "domain"
kernel.sched_cfs_bandwidth_slice_us = 5000
kernel.sched_child_runs_first = 0
kernel.sched_compat_yield = 0
kernel.sched_latency_ns = 6000000
kernel.sched_migration_cost_ns = 500000
kernel.sched_min_granularity_ns = 2000000
kernel.sched_nr_migrate = 32
kernel.sched_rr_timeslice_ms = 25
kernel.sched_rt_period_us = 1000000
kernel.sched_rt_runtime_us = 950000
kernel.sched_shares_window_ns = 10000000
kernel.sched_time_avg_ms = 1000
kernel.sched_tunable_scaling = 1
```

```
kernel.sched_wakeup_granularity_ns = 2500000
```

Note that variables ending with "_ns" and "_us" accept values in nanoseconds and microseconds, respectively.

A list of the most important task scheduler `sysctl` tuning variables (located at `/proc/sys/kernel/`) with a short description follows:

sched_child_runs_first

> A freshly forked child runs before the parent continues execution. Setting this parameter to `1` is beneficial for an application in which the child performs an execution after fork. For example `make` `-j<NO_CPUS>` performs better when sched_child_runs_first is turned off. The default value is `0`.

sched_compat_yield

> Enables the aggressive yield behavior of the old 0(1) scheduler. Java applications that use synchronization extensively perform better with this value set to `1`. Only use it when you see a drop in performance. The default value is `0`.
>
> Expect applications that depend on the sched_yield() syscall behavior to perform better with the value set to `1`.

sched_migration_cost_ns

> Amount of time after the last execution that a task is considered to be "cache hot" in migration decisions. A "hot" task is less likely to be migrated, so increasing this variable reduces task migrations. The default value is `500000` (ns).
>
> If the CPU idle time is higher than expected when there are runnable processes, try reducing this value. If tasks bounce between CPUs or nodes too often, try increasing it.

sched_latency_ns

> Targeted preemption latency for CPU bound tasks. Increasing this variable increases a CPU bound task's timeslice. A task's timeslice is its weighted fair share of the scheduling period:
> timeslice = scheduling period * (task's weight/total weight of tasks in the run queue)
> The task's weight depends on the task's nice level and the scheduling policy. Minimum task weight for a SCHED_OTHER task is 15, corresponding to nice 19. The maximum task weight is 88761, corresponding to nice -20.
> Timeslices become smaller as the load increases. When the number of runnable tasks exceeds `sched_latency_ns`/`sched_min_granularity_ns`, the slice becomes number_of_running_tasks * `sched_min_granularity_ns`. Prior to that, the slice is equal to `sched_latency_ns`.

This value also specifies the maximum amount of time during which a sleeping task is considered to be running for entitlement calculations. Increasing this variable increases the amount of time a waking task may consume before being preempted, thus increasing scheduler latency for CPU bound tasks. The default value is `6000000` (ns).

`sched_min_granularity_ns`

Minimal preemption granularity for CPU bound tasks. See `sched_latency_ns` for details. The default value is `4000000` (ns).

`sched_wakeup_granularity_ns`

The wake-up preemption granularity. Increasing this variable reduces wake-up preemption, reducing disturbance of compute bound tasks. Lowering it improves wake-up latency and throughput for latency critical tasks, particularly when a short duty cycle load component must compete with CPU bound components. The default value is `2500000` (ns).

 ## Warning: Setting the Right Wake-up Granularity Value

Settings larger than half of `sched_latency_ns` will result in no wake-up preemption. Short duty cycle tasks will be unable to compete with CPU hogs effectively.

`sched_rt_period_us`

Period over which real-time task bandwidth enforcement is measured. The default value is `1000000` (µs).

`sched_rt_runtime_us`

Quantum allocated to real-time tasks during sched_rt_period_us. Setting to -1 disables RT bandwidth enforcement. By default, RT tasks may consume 95%CPU/sec, thus leaving 5%CPU/sec or 0.05s to be used by SCHED_OTHER tasks. The default value is `950000` (µs).

`sched_nr_migrate`

Controls how many tasks can be moved across processors through migration software interrupts (softirq). If a large number of tasks is created by SCHED_OTHER policy, they will all be run on the same processor. The default value is `32`. Increasing this value gives a performance boost to large SCHED_OTHER threads at the expense of increased latencies for real-time tasks.

13.3.7 Debugging Interface and Scheduler Statistics

CFS comes with a new improved debugging interface, and provides runtime statistics information. Relevant files were added to the /proc file system, which can be examined simply with the **cat** or **less** command. A list of the related /proc files follows with their short description:

/proc/sched_debug

Contains the current values of all tunable variables (see *Section 13.3.6, "Runtime Tuning with* sysctl") that affect the task scheduler behavior, CFS statistics, and information about the run queue on all available processors.

```
root # cat /proc/sched_debug
Sched Debug Version: v0.11, 3.12.24-7-default #1
ktime                               : 23533900.395978
sched_clk                           : 23543587.726648
cpu_clk                             : 23533900.396165
jiffies                             : 4300775771
sched_clock_stable                  : 0

sysctl_sched
  .sysctl_sched_latency             : 6.000000
  .sysctl_sched_min_granularity     : 2.000000
  .sysctl_sched_wakeup_granularity  : 2.500000
  .sysctl_sched_child_runs_first    : 0
  .sysctl_sched_features            : 154871
  .sysctl_sched_tunable_scaling     : 1 (logaritmic)

cpu#0, 2666.762 MHz
  .nr_running          : 1
  .load                : 1024
  .nr_switches         : 1918946
[...]
cfs_rq[0]:/
  .exec_clock          : 170176.383770
  .MIN_vruntime        : 0.000001
  .min_vruntime        : 347375.854324
  .max_vruntime        : 0.000001
```

```
[...]
rt_rq[0]:/
  .rt_nr_running              : 0
  .rt_throttled               : 0
  .rt_time                    : 0.000000
  .rt_runtime                 : 950.000000

runnable tasks:
  task   PID        tree-key switches prio  exec-runtime  sum-exec sum-sleep
-----------------------------------------------------------------------------
R  cat 21772 347375.854324        2  120 347375.854324  0.488560 0.000000 0 /
```

/proc/schedstat

Displays statistics relevant to the current run queue. Also domain-specific statistics for SMP systems are displayed for all connected processors. Because the output format is not user-friendly, read the contents of /usr/src/linux/Documentation/scheduler/sched-stats.txt for more information.

/proc/*PID*/sched

Displays scheduling information on the process with id *PID*.

```
root # cat /proc/$(pidof gdm)/sched
gdm (744, #threads: 3)
----------------------------------------------------------------
se.exec_start                        :      8888.758381
se.vruntime                          :      6062.853815
se.sum_exec_runtime                  :         7.836043
se.statistics.wait_start             :         0.000000
se.statistics.sleep_start            :      8888.758381
se.statistics.block_start            :         0.000000
se.statistics.sleep_max              :      1965.987638
[...]
se.avg.decay_count                   :             8477
policy                               :                0
prio                                 :              120
clock-delta                          :              128
mm->numa_scan_seq                    :                0
```

```
numa_migrations, 0
numa_faults_memory, 0, 0, 1, 0, -1
numa_faults_memory, 1, 0, 0, 0, -1
```

13.4 For More Information

To get a compact knowledge about Linux kernel task scheduling, you need to explore several information sources. Here are some:

- For task scheduler System Calls description, see the relevant manual page (for example **man 2 sched_setaffinity**).

- General information on scheduling is described in Scheduling [http://en.wikipedia.org/wiki/Scheduling_(computing)] wiki page.

- A useful lecture on Linux scheduler policy and algorithm is available in http://www.inf.fu-berlin.de/lehre/SS01/OS/Lectures/Lecture08.pdf.

- A good overview of Linux process scheduling is given in *Linux Kernel Development* by Robert Love (ISBN-10: 0-672-32512-8). See http://www.informit.com/articles/article.aspx?p=101760.

- A very comprehensive overview of the Linux kernel internals is given in *Understanding the Linux Kernel* by Daniel P. Bovet and Marco Cesati (ISBN 978-0-596-00565-8).

- Technical information about task scheduler is covered in files under /usr/src/linux/Documentation/scheduler.

14 Tuning the Memory Management Subsystem

To understand and tune the memory management behavior of the kernel, it is important to first have an overview of how it works and cooperates with other subsystems.

The memory management subsystem, also called the virtual memory manager, will subsequently be called "VM". The role of the VM is to manage the allocation of physical memory (RAM) for the entire kernel and user programs. It is also responsible for providing a virtual memory environment for user processes (managed via POSIX APIs with Linux extensions). Finally, the VM is responsible for freeing up RAM when there is a shortage, either by trimming caches or swapping out "anonymous" memory.

The most important thing to understand when examining and tuning VM is how its caches are managed. The basic goal of the VM's caches is to minimize the cost of I/O as generated by swapping and file system operations (including network file systems). This is achieved by avoiding I/O completely, or by submitting I/O in better patterns.

Free memory will be used and filled up by these caches as required. The more memory is available for caches and anonymous memory, the more effectively caches and swapping will operate. However, if a memory shortage is encountered, caches will be trimmed or memory will be swapped out.

For a particular workload, the first thing that can be done to improve performance is to increase memory and reduce the frequency that memory must be trimmed or swapped. The second thing is to change the way caches are managed by changing kernel parameters.

Finally, the workload itself should be examined and tuned as well. If an application is allowed to run more processes or threads, effectiveness of VM caches can be reduced, if each process is operating in its own area of the file system. Memory overheads are also increased. If applications allocate their own buffers or caches, larger caches will mean that less memory is available for VM caches. However, more processes and threads can mean more opportunity to overlap and pipeline I/O, and may take better advantage of multiple cores. Experimentation will be required for the best results.

14.1 Memory Usage

Memory allocations in general can be characterized as "pinned" (also known as "unreclaimable"), "reclaimable" or "swappable".

14.1.1 Anonymous Memory

Anonymous memory tends to be program heap and stack memory (for example, `>malloc()`). It is reclaimable, except in special cases such as `mlock` or if there is no available swap space. Anonymous memory must be written to swap before it can be reclaimed. Swap I/O (both swapping in and swapping out pages) tends to be less efficient than pagecache I/O, because of allocation and access patterns.

14.1.2 Pagecache

A cache of file data. When a file is read from disk or network, the contents are stored in pagecache. No disk or network access is required, if the contents are up-to-date in pagecache. tmpfs and shared memory segments count toward pagecache.

When a file is written to, the new data is stored in pagecache before being written back to a disk or the network (making it a write-back cache). When a page has new data not written back yet, it is called "dirty". Pages not classified as dirty are "clean". Clean pagecache pages can be reclaimed if there is a memory shortage by simply freeing them. Dirty pages must first be made clean before being reclaimed.

14.1.3 Buffercache

This is a type of pagecache for block devices (for example, /dev/sda). A file system typically uses the buffercache when accessing its on-disk metadata structures such as inode tables, allocation bitmaps, and so forth. Buffercache can be reclaimed similarly to pagecache.

14.1.4 Buffer Heads

Buffer heads are small auxiliary structures that tend to be allocated upon pagecache access. They can generally be reclaimed easily when the pagecache or buffercache pages are clean.

14.1.5 Writeback

As applications write to files, the pagecache (and buffercache) becomes dirty. When pages have been dirty for a given amount of time, or when the amount of dirty memory reaches a specified number of pages in bytes (*vm.dirty_background_bytes*), the kernel begins writeback. Flusher threads perform writeback in the background and allow applications to continue running. If the I/O cannot keep up with applications dirtying pagecache, and dirty data reaches a critical setting (*vm.dirty_bytes*), then applications begin to be throttled to prevent dirty data exceeding this threshold.

14.1.6   Readahead

The VM monitors file access patterns and may attempt to perform readahead. Readahead reads pages into the pagecache from the file system that have not been requested yet. It is done to allow fewer, larger I/O requests to be submitted (more efficient). And for I/O to be pipelined (I/O performed at the same time as the application is running).

14.1.7   VFS caches

14.1.7.1   Inode Cache

This is an in-memory cache of the inode structures for each file system. These contain attributes such as the file size, permissions and ownership, and pointers to the file data.

14.1.7.2   Directory Entry Cache

This is an in-memory cache of the directory entries in the system. These contain a name (the name of a file), the inode which it refers to, and children entries. This cache is used when traversing the directory structure and accessing a file by name.

14.2   Reducing Memory Usage

14.2.1   Reducing malloc (Anonymous) Usage

Applications running on SUSE Linux Enterprise Server 12 SP1 can allocate more memory compared to SUSE Linux Enterprise Server 10. This is because of `glibc` changing its default behavior while allocating userspace memory. See http://www.gnu.org/s/libc/manual/html_node/Malloc-Tunable-Parameters.html for explanation of these parameters.

To restore a SUSE Linux Enterprise Server 10-like behavior, M_MMAP_THRESHOLD should be set to 128*1024. This can be done with mallopt() call from the application, or via setting MALLOC_MMAP_THRESHOLD environment variable before running the application.

14.2.2   Reducing Kernel Memory Overheads

Kernel memory that is reclaimable (caches, described above) will be trimmed automatically during memory shortages. Most other kernel memory cannot be easily reduced but is a property of the workload given to the kernel.

Reducing the requirements of the userspace workload will reduce the kernel memory usage (fewer processes, fewer open files and sockets, etc.)

14.2.3   Memory Controller (Memory Cgroups)

If the memory cgroups feature is not needed, it can be switched off by passing cgroup_disable=memory on the kernel command line, reducing memory consumption of the kernel a bit.

14.3   Virtual Memory Manager (VM) Tunable Parameters

When tuning the VM it should be understood that some changes will take time to affect the workload and take full effect. If the workload changes throughout the day, it may behave very differently at different times. A change that increases throughput under some conditions may decrease it under other conditions.

14.3.1 Reclaim Ratios

`/proc/sys/vm/swappiness`

This control is used to define how aggressively the kernel swaps out anonymous memory relative to pagecache and other caches. Increasing the value increases the amount of swapping. The default value is `60`.

Swap I/O tends to be much less efficient than other I/O. However, some pagecache pages will be accessed much more frequently than less used anonymous memory. The right balance should be found here.

If swap activity is observed during slowdowns, it may be worth reducing this parameter. If there is a lot of I/O activity and the amount of pagecache in the system is rather small, or if there are large dormant applications running, increasing this value might improve performance.

Note that the more data is swapped out, the longer the system will take to swap data back in when it is needed.

`/proc/sys/vm/vfs_cache_pressure`

This variable controls the tendency of the kernel to reclaim the memory which is used for caching of VFS caches, versus pagecache and swap. Increasing this value increases the rate at which VFS caches are reclaimed.

It is difficult to know when this should be changed, other than by experimentation. The **slabtop** command (part of the package `procps`) shows top memory objects used by the kernel. The vfs caches are the "dentry" and the "*_inode_cache" objects. If these are consuming a large amount of memory in relation to pagecache, it may be worth trying to increase pressure. Could also help to reduce swapping. The default value is `100`.

`/proc/sys/vm/min_free_kbytes`

This controls the amount of memory that is kept free for use by special reserves including "atomic" allocations (those which cannot wait for reclaim). This should not normally be lowered unless the system is being very carefully tuned for memory usage (normally useful for embedded rather than server applications). If "page allocation failure" messages and stack traces are frequently seen in logs, min_free_kbytes could be increased until the errors disappear. There is no need for concern, if these messages are very infrequent. The default value depends on the amount of RAM.

14.3.2 Writeback Parameters

One important change in writeback behavior since SUSE Linux Enterprise Server 10 is that modification to file-backed mmap() memory is accounted immediately as dirty memory (and subject to writeback). Whereas previously it would only be subject to writeback after it was unmapped, upon an msync() system call, or under heavy memory pressure.

Some applications do not expect mmap modifications to be subject to such writeback behavior, and performance can be reduced. Berkeley DB (and applications using it) is one known example that can cause problems. Increasing writeback ratios and times can improve this type of slowdown.

/proc/sys/vm/dirty_background_ratio

> This is the percentage of the total amount of free and reclaimable memory. When the amount of dirty pagecache exceeds this percentage, writeback threads start writing back dirty memory. The default value is 10 (%).

/proc/sys/vm/dirty_background_bytes

> This is the percentage of the total amount of dirty memory at which the background kernel flusher threads will start writeback. dirty_background_bytes is the counterpart of dirty_background_ratio. If one of them is set, the other one will automatically be read as 0.

/proc/sys/vm/dirty_ratio

> Similar percentage value as for dirty_background_ratio. When this is exceeded, applications that want to write to the pagecache are blocked and start performing writeback as well. The default value is 20 (%).

/proc/sys/vm/dirty_bytes

> Contains the amount of dirty memory (in percent) at which a process generating disk writes will itself start writeback. The minimum value allowed for dirty_bytes is two pages (in bytes); any value lower than this limit will be ignored and the old configuration will be retained.
>
> dirty_bytes is the counterpart of dirty_ratio. If one of them is set, the other one will automatically be read as 0.

`/proc/sys/vm/dirty_expires`

> Data which has been dirty in-memory for longer than this interval will be written out next time a flusher thread wakes up. Expiration is measured based on the modification time of a file's inode. Therefore, multiple dirtied pages from the same file will all be written when the interval is exceeded.

`dirty_background_ratio` and `dirty_ratio` together determine the pagecache writeback behavior. If these values are increased, more dirty memory is kept in the system for a longer time. With more dirty memory allowed in the system, the chance to improve throughput by avoiding writeback I/O and to submitting more optimal I/O patterns increases. However, more dirty memory can either harm latency when memory needs to be reclaimed or at points of data integrity ("sync points") when it needs to be written back to disk.

14.3.3 Timing Differences of I/O Writes between SUSE Linux Enterprise 12 and SUSE Linux Enterprise 11

The system is required to limit what percentage of the system's memory contains file-backed data that needs writing to disk. This guarantees that the system can always allocate the necessary data structures to complete I/O. The maximum amount of memory that may be dirty and requires writing at any given time is controlled by `vm.dirty_ratio` (`/proc/sys/vm/dirty_ratio`). The defaults are:

```
SLE-11-SP3:      vm.dirty_ratio = 40
SLE-12:          vm.dirty_ratio = 20
```

The primary advantage of using the lower ratio in SUSE Linux Enterprise 12 is that page reclamation and allocation in low memory situations completes faster as there is a higher probability that old clean pages will be quickly found and discarded. The secondary advantage is that if all data on the system must be synchronized, then the time to complete the operation on SUSE Linux Enterprise 12 will be lower than SUSE Linux Enterprise 11 SP3 by default. Most workloads will not notice this change as data is synchronized with `fsync()` by the application or data is not dirtied quickly enough to hit the limits.

There are exceptions and if your application is affected by this, it will manifest as an unexpected stall during writes. To prove it is affected by dirty data rate limiting then monitor `/proc/PID_OF_APPLICATION/stack` and it will be observed that the application spends significant time in `balance_dirty_pages_ratelimited`. If this is observed and it is a problem, then increase the value of `vm.dirty_ratio` to 40 to restore the SUSE Linux Enterprise 11 SP3 behavior.

It is important to note that the overall I/O throughput is the same regardless of the setting. The only difference is the timing of when the I/O is queued.

This is an example of using **dd** to asynchronously write 30% of memory to disk which would happen to be affected by the change in `vm.dirty_ratio`:

```
root # MEMTOTAL_MBYTES=`free -m | grep Mem: | awk '{print $2}'`
root # sysctl vm.dirty_ratio=40
root # dd if=/dev/zero of=zerofile ibs=1048576 count=$((MEMTOTAL_MBYTES*30/100))
2507145216 bytes (2.5 GB) copied, 8.00153 s, 313 MB/s
root # sysctl vm.dirty_ratio=20
dd if=/dev/zero of=zerofile ibs=1048576 count=$((MEMTOTAL_MBYTES*30/100))
2507145216 bytes (2.5 GB) copied, 10.1593 s, 247 MB/s
```

Note that the parameter affects the time it takes for the command to complete and the apparent write speed of the device. With `dirty_ratio=40`, more of the data is cached and written to disk in the background by the kernel. It is very important to note that the speed of I/O is identical in both cases. To demonstrate, this is the result when **dd** synchronizes the data before exiting:

```
root # sysctl vm.dirty_ratio=40
root # dd if=/dev/zero of=zerofile ibs=1048576 count=$((MEMTOTAL_MBYTES*30/100))
 conv=fdatasync
2507145216 bytes (2.5 GB) copied, 21.0663 s, 119 MB/s
root # sysctl vm.dirty_ratio=20
root # dd if=/dev/zero of=zerofile ibs=1048576 count=$((MEMTOTAL_MBYTES*30/100))
 conv=fdatasync
2507145216 bytes (2.5 GB) copied, 21.7286 s, 115 MB/s
```

Note that `dirty_ratio` had almost no impact here and is within the natural variability of a command. Hence, `dirty_ratio` does not directly impact I/O performance but it may affect the apparent performance of a workload that writes data asynchronously without synchronizing.

14.3.4   Readahead parameters

`/sys/block/<bdev>/queue/read_ahead_kb`

> If one or more processes are sequentially reading a file, the kernel reads some data in advance (ahead) to reduce the amount of time that processes need to wait for data to be available. The actual amount of data being read in advance is computed dynamically, based on how much "sequential" the I/O seems to be. This parameter sets the maximum amount of data that the kernel reads ahead for a single file. If you observe that large sequential reads from a file are not fast enough, you can try increasing this value. Increasing it too far may result in readahead thrashing where pagecache used for readahead is reclaimed before it can be used, or slowdowns because of a large amount of useless I/O. The default value is 512 (KB).

14.3.5   Further VM Parameters

For the complete list of the VM tunable parameters, see `/usr/src/linux/Documentation/sysctl/vm.txt` (available after having installed the `kernel-source` package).

14.4   Monitoring VM Behavior

Some simple tools that can help monitor VM behavior:

1. vmstat: This tool gives a good overview of what the VM is doing. See *Section 2.1.1, "*`vmstat`*"* for details.

2. `/proc/meminfo`: This file gives a detailed breakdown of where memory is being used. See *Section 2.4.2, "Detailed Memory Usage: *`/proc/meminfo`*"* for details.

3. **slabtop**: This tool provides detailed information about kernel slab memory usage. buffer_head, dentry, inode_cache, ext3_inode_cache, etc. are the major caches. This command is available with the package `procps`.

15 Tuning the Network

The network subsystem is rather complex and its tuning highly depends on the system use scenario and also on external factors such as software clients or hardware components (switches, routers, or gateways) in your network. The Linux kernel aims more at reliability and low latency than low overhead and high throughput. Other settings can mean less security, but better performance.

15.1 Configurable Kernel Socket Buffers

Networking is largely based on the TCP/IP protocol and a socket interface for communication; for more information about TCP/IP, see *Book "Administration Guide", Chapter 19 "Basic Networking"*. The Linux kernel handles data it receives or sends via the socket interface in socket buffers. These kernel socket buffers are tunable.

 Important: TCP Autotuning

Since kernel version 2.6.17 full autotuning with 4 MB maximum buffer size exists. This means that manual tuning usually will not improve networking performance considerably. It is often the best not to touch the following variables, or, at least, to check the outcome of tuning efforts carefully.

If you update from an older kernel, it is recommended to remove manual TCP tunings in favor of the autotuning feature.

The special files in the /proc file system can modify the size and behavior of kernel socket buffers; for general information about the /proc file system, see *Section 2.6, "The /proc File System"*. Find networking related files in:

```
/proc/sys/net/core
/proc/sys/net/ipv4
/proc/sys/net/ipv6
```

General net variables are explained in the kernel documentation (linux/Documentation/sysctl/net.txt). Special ipv4 variables are explained in linux/Documentation/networking/ip-sysctl.txt and linux/Documentation/networking/ipvs-sysctl.txt.

In the `/proc` file system, for example, it is possible to either set the Maximum Socket Receive Buffer and Maximum Socket Send Buffer for all protocols, or both these options for the TCP protocol only (in `ipv4`) and thus overriding the setting for all protocols (in `core`).

`/proc/sys/net/ipv4/tcp_moderate_rcvbuf`

If `/proc/sys/net/ipv4/tcp_moderate_rcvbuf` is set to `1`, autotuning is active and buffer size is adjusted dynamically.

`/proc/sys/net/ipv4/tcp_rmem`

The three values setting the minimum, initial, and maximum size of the Memory Receive Buffer per connection. They define the actual memory usage, not only TCP window size.

`/proc/sys/net/ipv4/tcp_wmem`

The same as `tcp_rmem`, but for Memory Send Buffer per connection.

`/proc/sys/net/core/rmem_max`

Set to limit the maximum receive buffer size that applications can request.

`/proc/sys/net/core/wmem_max`

Set to limit the maximum send buffer size that applications can request.

Via `/proc` it is possible to disable TCP features that you do not need (all TCP features are switched on by default). For example, check the following files:

`/proc/sys/net/ipv4/tcp_timestamps`

TCP time stamps are defined in RFC1323.

`/proc/sys/net/ipv4/tcp_window_scaling`

TCP window scaling is also defined in RFC1323.

`/proc/sys/net/ipv4/tcp_sack`

Select acknowledgments (SACKS).

Use **sysctl** to read or write variables of the `/proc` file system. **sysctl** is preferable to **cat** (for reading) and **echo** (for writing), because it also reads settings from `/etc/sysctl.conf` and, thus, those settings survive reboots reliably. With **sysctl** you can read all variables and their values easily; as `root` use the following command to list TCP related settings:

```
sysctl -a | grep tcp
```

Note: Side-Effects of Tuning Network Variables

Tuning network variables can affect other system resources such as CPU or memory use.

15.2   Detecting Network Bottlenecks and Analyzing Network Traffic

Before starting with network tuning, it is important to isolate network bottlenecks and network traffic patterns. There are some tools that can help you with detecting those bottlenecks.

The following tools can help analyzing your network traffic: `netstat`, `tcpdump`, and `wireshark`. Wireshark is a network traffic analyzer.

15.3   Netfilter

The Linux firewall and masquerading features are provided by the Netfilter kernel modules. This is a highly configurable rule based framework. If a rule matches a packet, Netfilter accepts or denies it or takes special action ("target") as defined by rules such as address translation.

There are quite some properties Netfilter can take into account. Thus, the more rules are defined, the longer packet processing may last. Also advanced connection tracking could be rather expensive and, thus, slowing down overall networking.

When the kernel queue becomes full, all new packets are dropped, causing existing connections to fail. The 'fail-open' feature, available since SUSE Linux Enterprise Server 11 SP3, allows a user to temporarily disable the packet inspection and maintain the connectivity under heavy network traffic. For reference, see https://home.regit.org/netfilter-en/using-nfqueue-and-libnetfilter_queue/.

For more information, see the home page of the Netfilter and iptables project, http://www.netfilter.org

15.4 Improving the Network Performance with Receive Packet Steering (RPS)

Modern network interface devices can move so many packets that the host can become the limiting factor for achieving maximum performance. In order to keep up, the system must be able to distribute the work across multiple CPU cores.

Some modern network interfaces can help distribute the work to multiple CPU cores through the implementation of multiple transmission and multiple receive queues in hardware. However, others are only equipped with a single queue and the driver must deal with all incoming packets in a single, serialized stream. To work around this issue, the operating system must "parallelize" the stream to distribute the work across multiple CPUs. On SUSE Linux Enterprise Server this is done via Receive Packet Steering (RPS). RPS can also be used in virtual environments.

RPS creates a unique hash for each data stream using IP addresses and port numbers. The use of this hash ensures that packets for the same data stream are sent to the same CPU, which helps to increase performance.

RPS is configured per network device receive queue and interface. The configuration file names match the following scheme:

```
/sys/class/net/<device>/queues/<rx-queue>/rps_cpus
```

`<device>` stands for the network device, such as `eth0`, `eth1`. `<rx-queue>` stands for the receive queue, such as `rx-0`, `rx-1`.

If the network interface hardware only supports a single receive queue, only `rx-0` will exist. If it supports multiple receive queues, there will be an rx-`N` directory for each receive queue.

These configuration files contain a comma-delimited list of CPU bitmaps. By default, all bits are set to `0`. With this setting RPS is disabled and therefore the CPU that handles the interrupt will also process the packet queue.

To enable RPS and enable specific CPUs to process packets for the receive queue of the interface, set the value of their positions in the bitmap to `1`. For example, to enable CPUs 0-3 to process packets for the first receive queue for eth0, set the bit positions 0-3 to 1 in binary: `00001111`. This representation then needs to be converted to hex—which results in `F` in this case. Set this hex value with the following command:

```
echo "f" > /sys/class/net/eth0/queues/rx-0/rps_cpus
```

If you wanted to enable CPUs 8-15:

```
1111 1111 0000 0000 (binary)
15   15   0    0 (decimal)
F    F    0    0 (hex)
```

The command to set the hex value of `ff00` would be:

```
echo "ff00" > /sys/class/net/eth0/queues/rx-0/rps_cpus
```

On NUMA machines, best performance can be achieved by configuring RPS to use the CPUs on the same NUMA node as the interrupt for the interface's receive queue.

On non-NUMA machines, all CPUs can be used. If the interrupt rate is very high, excluding the CPU handling the network interface can boost performance. The CPU being used for the network interface can be determined from `/proc/interrupts`. For example:

```
root # cat /proc/interrupts
          CPU0      CPU1      CPU2      CPU3
...
 51:  113915241        0         0         0    Phys-fasteoi   eth0
...
```

In this case, `CPU 0` is the only CPU processing interrupts for `eth0`, since only `CPU0` contains a non-zero value.

On i586 and x86_64 platforms, **irqbalance** can be used to distribute hardware interrupts across CPUs. See **man 1 irqbalance** for more details.

15.5 For More Information

- Eduardo Ciliendo, Takechika Kunimasa: "Linux Performance and Tuning Guidelines" (2007), esp. sections 1.5, 3.5, and 4.7: http://www.redbooks.ibm.com/redpapers/abstracts/redp4285.html

- John Heffner, Matt Mathis: "Tuning TCP for Linux 2.4 and 2.6" (2006): http://www.psc.edu/networking/projects/tcptune/#Linux

VI Handling System Dumps

16 Tracing Tools

SUSE Linux Enterprise Server comes with several tools that help you obtain useful information about your system. You can use the information for various purposes, for example, to debug and find problems in your program, to discover places causing performance drops, or to trace a running process to find out what system resources it uses. Most of the tools are part of the installation media. In some cases, they need to be installed from the SUSE Software Development Kit, which is a separate download.

 Note: Tracing and Impact on Performance

While a running process is being monitored for system or library calls, the performance of the process is heavily reduced. You are advised to use tracing tools only for the time you need to collect the data.

16.1 Tracing System Calls with strace

The **strace** command traces system calls of a process and signals received by the process. **strace** can either run a new command and trace its system calls, or you can attach **strace** to an already running command. Each line of the command's output contains the system call name, followed by its arguments in parentheses and its return value.

To run a new command and start tracing its system calls, enter the command to be monitored as you normally do, and add **strace** at the beginning of the command line:

```
tux@mercury:~> strace ls
execve("/bin/ls", ["ls"], [/* 52 vars */]) = 0
brk(0)                                  = 0x618000
mmap(NULL, 4096, PROT_READ|PROT_WRITE, MAP_PRIVATE|MAP_ANONYMOUS, -1, 0) \
 = 0x7f9848667000
mmap(NULL, 4096, PROT_READ|PROT_WRITE, MAP_PRIVATE|MAP_ANONYMOUS, -1, 0) \
 = 0x7f9848666000
access("/etc/ld.so.preload", R_OK)      = -1 ENOENT \
(No such file or directory)
open("/etc/ld.so.cache", O_RDONLY)      = 3
fstat(3, {st_mode=S_IFREG|0644, st_size=200411, ...}) = 0
```

```
mmap(NULL, 200411, PROT_READ, MAP_PRIVATE, 3, 0) = 0x7f9848635000
close(3)                                = 0
open("/lib64/librt.so.1", O_RDONLY)     = 3
[...]
mmap(NULL, 4096, PROT_READ|PROT_WRITE, MAP_PRIVATE|MAP_ANONYMOUS, -1, 0) \
= 0x7fd780f79000
write(1, "Desktop\nDocuments\nbin\ninst-sys\n", 31Desktop
Documents
bin
inst-sys
) = 31
close(1)                                = 0
munmap(0x7fd780f79000, 4096)            = 0
close(2)                                = 0
exit_group(0)                           = ?
```

To attach **strace** to an already running process, you need to specify the -p with the process ID (PID) of the process that you want to monitor:

```
tux@mercury:~> strace -p `pidof cron`
 Process 1261 attached
 restart_syscall(<... resuming interrupted call ...>) = 0
  stat("/etc/localtime", {st_mode=S_IFREG|0644, st_size=2309, ...}) = 0
  select(5, [4], NULL, NULL, {0, 0})       = 0 (Timeout)
  socket(PF_LOCAL, SOCK_STREAM|SOCK_CLOEXEC|SOCK_NONBLOCK, 0) = 5
  connect(5, {sa_family=AF_LOCAL, sun_path="/var/run/nscd/socket"}, 110) = 0
  sendto(5, "\2\0\0\0\0\0\0\0\5\0\0\0root\0", 17, MSG_NOSIGNAL, NULL, 0) = 17
  poll([{fd=5, events=POLLIN|POLLERR|POLLHUP}], 1, 5000) = 1 ([{fd=5,
 revents=POLLIN|POLLHUP}])
  read(5, "\2\0\0\0\1\0\0\0\5\0\0\0\2\0\0\0\0\0\0\0\0\0\0\0\5\0\0\0\6\0\0\0"..., 36)
 = 36
  read(5, "root\0x\0root\0/root\0/bin/bash\0", 28) = 28
  close(5)                                 = 0
  rt_sigprocmask(SIG_BLOCK, [CHLD], [], 8) = 0
  rt_sigaction(SIGCHLD, NULL, {0x7f772b9ea890, [], SA_RESTORER|SA_RESTART,
 0x7f772adf7880}, 8) = 0
```

```
 rt_sigprocmask(SIG_SETMASK, [], NULL, 8) = 0
 nanosleep({60, 0}, 0x7fff87d8c580)      = 0
 stat("/etc/localtime", {st_mode=S_IFREG|0644, st_size=2309, ...}) = 0
 select(5, [4], NULL, NULL, {0, 0})       = 0 (Timeout)
 socket(PF_LOCAL, SOCK_STREAM|SOCK_CLOEXEC|SOCK_NONBLOCK, 0) = 5
 connect(5, {sa_family=AF_LOCAL, sun_path="/var/run/nscd/socket"}, 110) = 0
 sendto(5, "\2\0\0\0\0\0\0\5\0\0\0root\0", 17, MSG_NOSIGNAL, NULL, 0) = 17
 poll([{fd=5, events=POLLIN|POLLERR|POLLHUP}], 1, 5000) = 1 ([{fd=5,
 revents=POLLIN|POLLHUP}])
 read(5, "\2\0\0\0\1\0\0\0\5\0\0\0\2\0\0\0\0\0\0\0\0\0\0\0\5\0\0\0\6\0\0\0"..., 36)
= 36
 read(5, "root\0x\0root\0/root\0/bin/bash\0", 28) = 28
 close(5)
 [...]
```

The `-e` option understands several sub-options and arguments. For example, to trace all attempts to open or write to a particular file, use the following:

```
tux@mercury:~> strace -e trace=open,write ls ~
open("/etc/ld.so.cache", O_RDONLY)       = 3
open("/lib64/librt.so.1", O_RDONLY)      = 3
open("/lib64/libselinux.so.1", O_RDONLY) = 3
open("/lib64/libacl.so.1", O_RDONLY)     = 3
open("/lib64/libc.so.6", O_RDONLY)       = 3
open("/lib64/libpthread.so.0", O_RDONLY) = 3
[...]
open("/usr/lib/locale/cs_CZ.utf8/LC_CTYPE", O_RDONLY) = 3
open(".", O_RDONLY|O_NONBLOCK|O_DIRECTORY|O_CLOEXEC) = 3
write(1, "addressbook.db.bak\nbin\ncxoffice\n"..., 311) = 311
```

To trace only network related system calls, use `-e trace=network`:

```
tux@mercury:~> strace -e trace=network -p 26520
Process 26520 attached - interrupt to quit
socket(PF_NETLINK, SOCK_RAW, 0)          = 50
bind(50, {sa_family=AF_NETLINK, pid=0, groups=00000000}, 12) = 0
getsockname(50, {sa_family=AF_NETLINK, pid=26520, groups=00000000}, \
```

```
[12]) = 0
sendto(50, "\24\0\0\0\26\0\1\3~p\315K\0\0\0\0\0\0\0\0", 20, 0,
{sa_family=AF_NETLINK, pid=0, groups=00000000}, 12) = 20
[...]
```

The -c calculates the time the kernel spent on each system call:

```
tux@mercury:~> strace -c find /etc -name xorg.conf
/etc/X11/xorg.conf
% time     seconds  usecs/call     calls    errors syscall
------ ----------- ----------- --------- --------- ----------------
 32.38    0.000181         181         1           execve
 22.00    0.000123           0       576           getdents64
 19.50    0.000109           0       917        31 open
 19.14    0.000107           0       888           close
  4.11    0.000023           2        10           mprotect
  0.00    0.000000           0         1           write
[...]
  0.00    0.000000           0         1           getrlimit
  0.00    0.000000           0         1           arch_prctl
  0.00    0.000000           0         3         1 futex
  0.00    0.000000           0         1           set_tid_address
  0.00    0.000000           0         4           fadvise64
  0.00    0.000000           0         1           set_robust_list
------ ----------- ----------- --------- --------- ----------------
100.00    0.000559                  3633        33 total
```

To trace all child processes of a process, use -f:

```
tux@mercury:~> strace -f rcapache2 status
execve("/usr/sbin/rcapache2", ["rcapache2", "status"], [/* 81 vars */]) = 0
brk(0)                                  = 0x69e000
mmap(NULL, 4096, PROT_READ|PROT_WRITE, MAP_PRIVATE|MAP_ANONYMOUS, -1, 0) \
= 0x7f3bb553b000
mmap(NULL, 4096, PROT_READ|PROT_WRITE, MAP_PRIVATE|MAP_ANONYMOUS, -1, 0) \
= 0x7f3bb553a000
[...]
```

```
[pid  4823] rt_sigprocmask(SIG_SETMASK, [],  <unfinished ...>
[pid  4822] close(4 <unfinished ...>
[pid  4823] <... rt_sigprocmask resumed> NULL, 8) = 0
[pid  4822] <... close resumed> )        = 0
[...]
[pid  4825] mprotect(0x7fc42cbbd000, 16384, PROT_READ) = 0
[pid  4825] mprotect(0x60a000, 4096, PROT_READ) = 0
[pid  4825] mprotect(0x7fc42cde4000, 4096, PROT_READ) = 0
[pid  4825] munmap(0x7fc42cda2000, 261953) = 0
[...]
[pid  4830] munmap(0x7fb1fff10000, 261953) = 0
[pid  4830] rt_sigprocmask(SIG_BLOCK, NULL, [], 8) = 0
[pid  4830] open("/dev/tty", O_RDWR|O_NONBLOCK) = 3
[pid  4830] close(3)
[...]
read(255, "\n\n# Inform the caller not only v"..., 8192) = 73
rt_sigprocmask(SIG_BLOCK, NULL, [], 8)  = 0
rt_sigprocmask(SIG_BLOCK, NULL, [], 8)  = 0
exit_group(0)
```

If you need to analyze the output of **strace** and the output messages are too long to be inspected directly in the console window, use -o. In that case, unnecessary messages, such as information about attaching and detaching processes, are suppressed. You can also suppress these messages (normally printed on the standard output) with -q. To prepend time stamps to each line with a system call, use -t:

```
tux@mercury:~> strace -t -o strace_sleep.txt sleep 1; more strace_sleep.txt
08:44:06 execve("/bin/sleep", ["sleep", "1"], [/* 81 vars */]) = 0
08:44:06 brk(0)                    = 0x606000
08:44:06 mmap(NULL, 4096, PROT_READ|PROT_WRITE, MAP_PRIVATE|MAP_ANONYMOUS, \
-1, 0) = 0x7f8e78cc5000
[...]
08:44:06 close(3)                  = 0
08:44:06 nanosleep({1, 0}, NULL)   = 0
08:44:07 close(1)                  = 0
08:44:07 close(2)                  = 0
```

```
08:44:07 exit_group(0)                    = ?
```

The behavior and output format of strace can be largely controlled. For more information, see the relevant manual page (man 1 strace).

16.2 Tracing Library Calls with ltrace

ltrace traces dynamic library calls of a process. It is used in a similar way to **strace**, and most of their parameters have a very similar or identical meaning. By default, **ltrace** uses `/etc/ltrace.conf` or `~/.ltrace.conf` configuration files. You can, however, specify an alternative one with the `-F config_file` option.

In addition to library calls, **ltrace** with the `-S` option can trace system calls as well:

```
tux@mercury:~> ltrace -S -o ltrace_find.txt find /etc -name \
xorg.conf; more ltrace_find.txt
SYS_brk(NULL)                                  = 0x00628000
SYS_mmap(0, 4096, 3, 34, 0xffffffff)           = 0x7f1327ea1000
SYS_mmap(0, 4096, 3, 34, 0xffffffff)           = 0x7f1327ea0000
[...]
fnmatch("xorg.conf", "xorg.conf", 0)           = 0
free(0x0062db80)                               = <void>
__errno_location()                             = 0x7f1327e5d698
__ctype_get_mb_cur_max(0x7fff25227af0, 8192, 0x62e020, -1, 0) = 6
__ctype_get_mb_cur_max(0x7fff25227af0, 18, 0x7f1327e5d6f0, 0x7fff25227af0,
0x62e031) = 6
__fprintf_chk(0x7f1327821780, 1, 0x420cf7, 0x7fff25227af0, 0x62e031
<unfinished ...>
SYS_fstat(1, 0x7fff25227230)                   = 0
SYS_mmap(0, 4096, 3, 34, 0xffffffff)           = 0x7f1327e72000
SYS_write(1, "/etc/X11/xorg.conf\n", 19)       = 19
[...]
```

You can change the type of traced events with the `-e` option. The following example prints library calls related to `fnmatch` and `strlen` functions:

```
tux@mercury:~> ltrace -e fnmatch,strlen find /etc -name xorg.conf
```

```
[...]
fnmatch("xorg.conf", "xorg.conf", 0)              = 0
strlen("Xresources")                              = 10
strlen("Xresources")                              = 10
strlen("Xresources")                              = 10
fnmatch("xorg.conf", "Xresources", 0)             = 1
strlen("xorg.conf.install")                       = 17
[...]
```

To display only the symbols included in a specific library, use -l /path/to/library:

```
tux@mercury:~> ltrace -l /lib64/librt.so.1 sleep 1
clock_gettime(1, 0x7fff4b5c34d0, 0, 0, 0)                   = 0
clock_gettime(1, 0x7fff4b5c34c0, 0xffffffffff600180, -1, 0) = 0
+++ exited (status 0) +++
```

You can make the output more readable by indenting each nested call by the specified number of space with the -n num_of_spaces.

16.3 Debugging and Profiling with Valgrind

Valgrind is a set of tools to debug and profile your programs so that they can run faster and with less errors. Valgrind can detect problems related to memory management and threading, or can also serve as a framework for building new debugging tools.

16.3.1 Installation

Valgrind is not shipped with standard SUSE Linux Enterprise Server distribution. To install it on your system, you need to obtain SUSE Software Development Kit, and either install it and run

zypper install valgrind

or browse through the SUSE Software Development Kit directory tree, locate the Valgrind package and install it with

rpm -i valgrind-version_architecture.rpm

The SDK is a module for SUSE Linux Enterprise and is available via an online channel from the SUSE Customer Center. Alternatively download it from http://download.suse.com/. (Search for `SUSE Linux Enterprise Software Development Kit`). Refer to *Book "Deployment Guide", Chapter 9 "Installing Modules, Extensions, and Third Party Add-On Products"* for details.

16.3.2   Supported Architectures

SUSE Linux Enterprise Server supports Valgrind on the following architectures:

- x86_64

- ppc64

- z Systems

16.3.3   General Information

The main advantage of Valgrind is that it works with existing compiled executables. You do not need to recompile or modify your programs to use it. Run Valgrind like this:

valgrind *valgrind_options* your-prog *your-program-options*

Valgrind consists of several tools, and each provides specific functionality. Information in this section is general and valid regardless of the used tool. The most important configuration option is `--tool`. This option tells Valgrind which tool to run. If you omit this option, `memcheck` is selected by default. For example, if you want to run **find** `~` `-name` .bashrc with Valgrind's `memcheck` tools, enter the following in the command line:

valgrind `--tool` = *memcheck* find ~ -name .bashrc

A list of standard Valgrind tools with a brief description follows:

memcheck

Detects memory errors. It helps you tune your programs to behave correctly.

cachegrind

Profiles cache prediction. It helps you tune your programs to run faster.

callgrind

Works in a similar way to `cachegrind` but also gathers additional cache-profiling information.

`exp-drd`

Detects thread errors. It helps you tune your multi-threaded programs to behave correctly.

`helgrind`

Another thread error detector. Similar to `exp-drd` but uses different techniques for problem analysis.

`massif`

A heap profiler. Heap is an area of memory used for dynamic memory allocation. This tool helps you tune your program to use less memory.

`lackey`

An example tool showing instrumentation basics.

16.3.4   Default Options

Valgrind can read options at start-up. There are three places which Valgrind checks:

1. The file `.valgrindrc` in the home directory of the user who runs Valgrind.

2. The environment variable `$VALGRIND_OPTS`

3. The file `.valgrindrc` in the current directory where Valgrind is run from.

These resources are parsed exactly in this order, while later given options take precedence over earlier processed options. Options specific to a particular Valgrind tool must be prefixed with the tool name and a colon. For example, if you want `cachegrind` to always write profile data to the `/tmp/cachegrind_PID.log`, add the following line to the `.valgrindrc` file in your home directory:

```
--cachegrind:cachegrind-out-file=/tmp/cachegrind_%p.log
```

16.3.5   How Valgrind Works

Valgrind takes control of your executable before it starts. It reads debugging information from the executable and related shared libraries. The executable's code is redirected to the selected Valgrind tool, and the tool adds its own code to handle its debugging. Then the code is handed back to the Valgrind core and the execution continues.

For example, `memcheck` adds its code, which checks every memory access. As a consequence, the program runs much slower than in the native execution environment.

Valgrind simulates every instruction of your program. Therefore, it not only checks the code of your program, but also all related libraries (including the C library), libraries used for graphical environment, and so on. If you try to detect errors with Valgrind, it also detects errors in associated libraries (like C, X11, or Gtk libraries). Because you probably do not need these errors, Valgrind can selectively, suppress these error messages to suppression files. The `--gen-suppressions=yes` tells Valgrind to report these suppressions which you can copy to a file.

You should supply a real executable (machine code) as a Valgrind argument. If your application is run, for example, from a shell or Perl script, you will by mistake get error reports related to **/bin/sh** (or **/usr/bin/perl**). In such cases, you can use `--trace-children=yes` to work around this issue. However, using the executable itself will avoid any confusion over this issue.

16.3.6   Messages

During its runtime, Valgrind reports messages with detailed errors and important events. The following example explains the messages:

```
tux@mercury:~> valgrind --tool=memcheck find ~ -name .bashrc
[...]
==6558== Conditional jump or move depends on uninitialised value(s)
==6558==    at 0x400AE79: _dl_relocate_object (in /lib64/ld-2.11.1.so)
==6558==    by 0x4003868: dl_main (in /lib64/ld-2.11.1.so)
[...]
==6558== Conditional jump or move depends on uninitialised value(s)
==6558==    at 0x400AE82: _dl_relocate_object (in /lib64/ld-2.11.1.so)
==6558==    by 0x4003868: dl_main (in /lib64/ld-2.11.1.so)
[...]
==6558== ERROR SUMMARY: 2 errors from 2 contexts (suppressed: 0 from 0)
==6558== malloc/free: in use at exit: 2,228 bytes in 8 blocks.
==6558== malloc/free: 235 allocs, 227 frees, 489,675 bytes allocated.
==6558== For counts of detected errors, rerun with: -v
==6558== searching for pointers to 8 not-freed blocks.
==6558== checked 122,584 bytes.
==6558==
```

```
==6558== LEAK SUMMARY:
==6558==    definitely lost: 0 bytes in 0 blocks.
==6558==     possibly lost: 0 bytes in 0 blocks.
==6558==    still reachable: 2,228 bytes in 8 blocks.
==6558==         suppressed: 0 bytes in 0 blocks.
==6558== Rerun with --leak-check=full to see details of leaked memory.
```

The `==6558==` introduces Valgrind's messages and contains the process ID number (PID). You can easily distinguish Valgrind's messages from the output of the program itself, and decide which messages belong to a particular process.

To make Valgrind's messages more detailed, use `-v` or even `-v -v`.

You can make Valgrind send its messages to three different places:

1. By default, Valgrind sends its messages to the file descriptor 2, which is the standard error output. You can tell Valgrind to send its messages to any other file descriptor with the `--log-fd=file_descriptor_number` option.

2. The second and probably more useful way is to send Valgrind's messages to a file with `--log-file=filename`. This option accepts several variables, for example, `%p` gets replaced with the PID of the currently profiled process. This way you can send messages to different files based on their PID. `%q{env_var}` is replaced with the value of the related `env_var` environment variable.

   The following example checks for possible memory errors during the Apache Web server restart, while following children processes and writing detailed Valgrind's messages to separate files distinguished by the current process PID:

```
tux@mercury:~> valgrind -v --tool=memcheck --trace-children=yes \
--log-file=valgrind_pid_%p.log rcapache2 restart
```

This process created 52 log files in the testing system, and took 75 seconds instead of the usual 7 seconds needed to run **sudo systemctl restart apache2** without Valgrind, which is approximately 10 times more.

```
tux@mercury:~> ls -1 valgrind_pid_*log
valgrind_pid_11780.log
valgrind_pid_11782.log
valgrind_pid_11783.log
```

```
[...]
valgrind_pid_11860.log
valgrind_pid_11862.log
valgrind_pid_11863.log
```

3. You may also prefer to send the Valgrind's messages over the network. You need to specify the `aa.bb.cc.dd` IP address and `port_num` port number of the network socket with the `--log-socket=aa.bb.cc.dd:port_num` option. If you omit the port number, 1500 will be used.

   It is useless to send Valgrind's messages to a network socket if no application is capable of receiving them on the remote machine. That is why **valgrind-listener**, a simple listener, is shipped together with Valgrind. It accepts connections on the specified port and copies everything it receives to the standard output.

16.3.7   Error Messages

Valgrind remembers all error messages, and if it detects a new error, the error is compared against old error messages. This way Valgrind checks for duplicate error messages. In case of a duplicate error, it is recorded but no message is shown. This mechanism prevents you from being overwhelmed by millions of duplicate errors.

The `-v` option will add a summary of all reports (sorted by their total count) to the end of the Valgrind's execution output. Moreover, Valgrind stops collecting errors if it detects either 1000 different errors, or 10 000 000 errors in total. If you want to suppress this limit and wish to see all error messages, use `--error-limit=no`.

Some errors usually cause other ones. Therefore, fix errors in the same order as they appear and re-check the program continuously.

16.4 For More Information

- For a complete list of options related to the described tracing tools, see the corresponding man page (`man 1 strace`, `man 1 ltrace`, and `man 1 valgrind`).

- To describe advanced usage of Valgrind is beyond the scope of this document. It is very well documented, see Valgrind User Manual [http://valgrind.org/docs/manual/manual.html]. These pages are indispensable if you need more advanced information on Valgrind or the usage and purpose of its standard tools.

17 Kexec and Kdump

Kexec is a tool to boot to another kernel from the currently running one. You can perform faster system reboots without any hardware initialization. You can also prepare the system to boot to another kernel if the system crashes.

17.1 Introduction

With Kexec, you can replace the running kernel with another one without a hard reboot. The tool is useful for several reasons:

- Faster system rebooting
  If you need to reboot the system frequently, Kexec can save you significant time.

- Avoiding unreliable firmware and hardware
  Computer hardware is complex and serious problems may occur during the system start-up. You cannot always replace unreliable hardware immediately. Kexec boots the kernel to a controlled environment with the hardware already initialized. The risk of unsuccessful system start is then minimized.

- Saving the dump of a crashed kernel
  Kexec preserves the contents of the physical memory. After the *production* kernel fails, the *capture* kernel (an additional kernel running in a reserved memory range) saves the state of the failed kernel. The saved image can help you with the subsequent analysis.

- Booting without GRUB 2 or ELILO configuration
  When the system boots a kernel with Kexec, it skips the boot loader stage. The normal booting procedure can fail because of an error in the boot loader configuration. With Kexec, you do not depend on a working boot loader configuration.

17.2 Required Packages

To use Kexec on SUSE® Linux Enterprise Server to speed up reboots or avoid potential hardware problems, make sure that the package `kexec-tools` is installed. It contains a script called **kexec-bootloader**, which reads the boot loader configuration and runs Kexec using the same kernel options as the normal boot loader.

To set up an environment that helps you obtain debug information in case of a kernel crash, make sure that the package `makedumpfile` is installed.

The preferred method of using Kdump in SUSE Linux Enterprise Server is through the YaST Kdump module. To use the YaST module, make sure that the package `yast2-kdump` is installed.

17.3 Kexec Internals

The most important component of Kexec is the `/sbin/kexec` command. You can load a kernel with Kexec in two different ways:

- Load the kernel to the address space of a production kernel for a regular reboot:

```
root # kexec -l kernel_image
```

  You can later boot to this kernel with **kexec** -e.

- Load the kernel to a reserved area of memory:

```
root # kexec -p kernel_image
```

  This kernel will be booted automatically when the system crashes.

If you want to boot another kernel and preserve the data of the production kernel when the system crashes, you need to reserve a dedicated area of the system memory. The production kernel never loads to this area because it must be always available. It is used for the capture kernel so that the memory pages of the production kernel can be preserved.

To reserve the area, append the option `crashkernel` to the boot command line of the production kernel. To determine the necessary values for `crashkernel`, follow the instructions in *Section 17.4, "Calculating `crashkernel` Allocation Size"*.

Note that this is not a parameter of the capture kernel. The capture kernel does not use Kexec.

The capture kernel is loaded to the reserved area and waits for the kernel to crash. Then, Kdump tries to invoke the capture kernel because the production kernel is no longer reliable at this stage. This means that even Kdump can fail.

To load the capture kernel, you need to include the kernel boot parameters. Usually, the initial RAM file system is used for booting. You can specify it with `--initrd = filename`. With `--append = cmdline`, you append options to the command line of the kernel to boot.

It is helpful to include the command line of the production kernel if these options are necessary for the kernel to boot. You can simply copy the command line with `--append = "$(cat /proc/cmdline)"` or add more options with `--append = "$(cat /proc/cmdline) more_options"`.

You can always unload the previously loaded kernel. To unload a kernel that was loaded with the `-l` option, use the **kexec** `-u` command. To unload a crash kernel loaded with the `-p` option, use **kexec** `-p` `-u` command.

17.4 Calculating `crashkernel` Allocation Size

To use Kexec with a capture kernel and to use Kdump in any way, RAM needs to be allocated for the capture kernel. The allocation size depends on the expected hardware configuration of the computer, therefore you need to specify it.

The allocation size also depends on the hardware architecture of your computer. Make sure to follow the procedure intended for your system architecture.

PROCEDURE 17.1: ALLOCATION SIZE ON AMD64/INTEL 64

1. To find out the basis value for the computer, run the following in a terminal:

   ```
   root # kdumptool calibrate
   ```

   This command returns a list of values. All values are given in megabytes.

2. Write down the values of `Low` and `High`.

    Note: Significance of `Low` **and** `High` **Values**

   On AMD64/Intel 64 computers, the `High` value stands for the memory reservation for all available memory. The `Low` value stands for the memory reservation in the DMA32 zone, that is, all the memory up to the 4 GB mark.

   If the computer has less than 4 GB of RAM, the `High` memory reservation is allocated and the `Low` memory reservation is ignored. If the computer has more than 4 GB of RAM, the `Low` memory reservation is allocated additionally.

3. Adapt the `High` value from the previous step for the number of LUN kernel paths (paths to storage devices) attached to the computer. A sensible value in megabytes can be calculated using this formula:

```
SIZE_HIGH = RECOMMENDATION + (LUNs / 2)
```

The following parameters are used in this formula:

- **SIZE_HIGH.** The resulting value for `High`.

- **RECOMMENDATION.** The value recommended by **kdumptool calibrate** for `High`.

- **LUNs.** The maximum number of LUN kernel paths that you expect to ever create on the computer. Exclude multipath devices from this number, as these are ignored.

4. If the drivers for your device make many reservations in the DMA32 zone, the `Low` value also needs to be adjusted. However, there is no simple formula to calculate these. Finding the right size can therefore be a process of trial and error.
   For the beginning, use the `Low` value recommended by **kdump calibrate**.

5. The values now need to be set in the correct location.

   If you are working on the command line
   Append the following kernel option to your boot loader configuration:

   ```
   crashkernel=SIZE_HIGH,high crashkernel=SIZE_LOW,low
   ```

   Replace the placeholders *SIZE_HIGH* and *SIZE_LOW* with the appropriate value from the previous steps and append the letter `M` (for megabytes).
   As an example, the following is valid:

   ```
   crashkernel=36M,high crashkernel=72M,low
   ```

   If you are working in YaST
   Set *Kdump Low Memory* to the determined `Low` value.
   Set *Kdump High Memory* to the determined `High` value.

PROCEDURE 17.2: ALLOCATION SIZE ON POWER AND Z SYSTEMS

1. To find out the basis value for the computer, run the following in a terminal:

   ```
   root # kdumptool calibrate
   ```

   This command returns a list of values. All values are given in megabytes.

2. Write down the value of Low.

3. Adapt the Low value from the previous step for the number of LUN kernel paths (paths to storage devices) attached to the computer. A sensible value in megabytes can be calculated using this formula:

```
SIZE_LOW = RECOMMENDATION + (LUNs / 2)
```

The following parameters are used in this formula:

- **SIZE_LOW.** The resulting value for Low.

- **RECOMMENDATION.** The value recommended by **kdumptool calibrate** for Low.

- **LUNs.** The maximum number of LUN kernel paths that you expect to ever create on the computer. Exclude multipath devices from this number, as these are ignored.

4. The values now need to be set in the correct location.

   If you are working on the command line
   Append the following kernel option to your boot loader configuration:

   ```
   crashkernel=SIZE_LOW
   ```

   Replace the placeholder *SIZE_LOW* with the appropriate value from the previous step and append the letter M (for megabytes).
   As an example, the following is valid:

   ```
   crashkernel=108M
   ```

   If you are working in YaST
   Set *Kdump Memory* to the determined Low value.

17.5 Basic Kexec Usage

To verify if your Kexec environment works properly, follow these steps:

1. Make sure no users are currently logged in and no important services are running on the system.

2. Log in as `root`.

3. Switch to the rescue target with **systemctl isolate rescue.target**

4. Load the new kernel to the address space of the production kernel with the following command:

```
root # kexec -l /boot/vmlinuz --append="$(cat /proc/cmdline)" \
--initrd=/boot/initrd
```

5. Unmount all mounted file systems except the root file system with:

```
umount -a
```

 Important: Unmounting the Root File System

Unmounting all file systems will most likely produce a `device is busy` warning message. The root file system cannot be unmounted if the system is running. Ignore the warning.

6. Remount the root file system in read-only mode:

```
root # mount -o remount,ro /
```

7. Initiate the reboot of the kernel that you loaded in *Step 4* with:

```
root # kexec -e
```

It is important to unmount the previously mounted disk volumes in read-write mode. The `reboot` system call acts immediately upon calling. Hard disk volumes mounted in read-write mode neither synchronize nor unmount automatically. The new kernel may find them "dirty". Read-only disk volumes and virtual file systems do not need to be unmounted. Refer to `/etc/mtab` to determine which file systems you need to unmount.

The new kernel previously loaded to the address space of the older kernel rewrites it and takes control immediately. It displays the usual start-up messages. When the new kernel boots, it skips all hardware and firmware checks. Make sure no warning messages appear. All file systems are supposed to be clean if they had been unmounted.

17.6 How to Configure Kexec for Routine Reboots

Kexec is often used for frequent reboots. For example, if it takes a long time to run through the hardware detection routines or if the start-up is not reliable.

Note that firmware and the boot loader are not used when the system reboots with Kexec. Any changes you make to the boot loader configuration will be ignored until the computer performs a hard reboot.

17.7 Basic Kdump Configuration

You can use Kdump to save kernel dumps. If the kernel crashes, it is useful to copy the memory image of the crashed environment to the file system. You can then debug the dump file to find the cause of the kernel crash. This is called "core dump".

Kdump works similarly to Kexec (see *Chapter 17, Kexec and Kdump*). The capture kernel is executed after the running production kernel crashes. The difference is that Kexec replaces the production kernel with the capture kernel. With Kdump, you still have access to the memory space of the crashed production kernel. You can save the memory snapshot of the crashed kernel in the environment of the Kdump kernel.

 Tip: Dumps over Network

In environments with limited local storage, you need to set up kernel dumps over the network. Kdump supports configuring the specified network interface and bringing it up via `initrd`. Both LAN and VLAN interfaces are supported. Specify the network interface and the mode (DHCP or static) either with YaST, or using the `KDUMP_NETCONFIG` option in the `/etc/sysconfig/kdump` file.

 Important: Target File System for Kdump Must Be Mounted During Configuration

When configuring Kdump, you can specify a location to which the dumped images will be saved (default: `/var/crash`). This location must be mounted when configuring Kdump, otherwise the configuration will fail.

17.7.1 Manual Kdump Configuration

Kdump reads its configuration from the `/etc/sysconfig/kdump` file. To make sure that Kdump works on your system, its default configuration is sufficient. To use Kdump with the default settings, follow these steps:

1. Determine the amount of memory needed for Kdump by following the instructions in *Section 17.4, "Calculating* `crashkernel` *Allocation Size"*. Make sure to set the kernel parameter `crashkernel`.

2. Reboot the computer.

3. Enable the Kdump service:

```
root # systemctl enable kdump
```

4. You can edit the options in `/etc/sysconfig/kdump`. Reading the comments will help you understand the meaning of individual options.

5. Execute the init script once with **sudo systemctl start kdump**, or reboot the system.

After configuring Kdump with the default values, check if it works as expected. Make sure that no users are currently logged in and no important services are running on your system. Then follow these steps:

1. Switch to the rescue target with **systemctl isolate rescue.target**

2. Unmount all the disk file systems except the root file system with:

```
root # umount -a
```

3. Remount the root file system in read-only mode:

```
root # mount -o remount,ro /
```

4. Invoke a "kernel panic" with the `procfs` interface to Magic SysRq keys:

```
root # echo c > /proc/sysrq-trigger
```

Important: Size of Kernel Dumps

The `KDUMP_KEEP_OLD_DUMPS` option controls the number of preserved kernel dumps (default is 5). Without compression, the size of the dump can take up to the size of the physical RAM memory. Make sure you have sufficient space on the `/var` partition.

The capture kernel boots and the crashed kernel memory snapshot is saved to the file system. The save path is given by the `KDUMP_SAVEDIR` option and it defaults to `/var/crash`. If `KDUMP_IMMEDIATE_REBOOT` is set to `yes`, the system automatically reboots the production kernel. Log in and check that the dump has been created under `/var/crash`.

17.7.2   YaST Configuration

To configure Kdump with YaST, you need to install the `yast2-kdump` package. Then either start the *Kernel Kdump* module in the *System* category of *YaST Control Center*, or enter **yast2 kdump** in the command line as `root`.

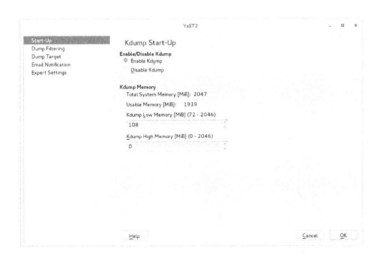

FIGURE 17.1: YAST KDUMP MODULE: START-UP PAGE

In the *Start-Up* window, select *Enable Kdump*.

The values for *Kdump Memory* are automatically generated the first time you open the window. However, that does not mean that they are always sufficient. To set the right values, follow the instructions in *Section 17.4, "Calculating* `crashkernel` *Allocation Size".*

YaST Configuration

Important: After Hardware Changes, Set *Kdump Memory* **Values Again**

If you have set up Kdump on a computer and later decide to change the amount of RAM or hard disks available to it, YaST will continue to display and use outdated memory values.

To work around this, determine the necessary memory again, as described in *Section 17.4, "Calculating* crashkernel *Allocation Size"*. Then set it manually in YaST.

Click *Dump Filtering* in the left pane, and check what pages to include in the dump. You do not need to include the following memory content to be able to debug kernel problems:

- Pages filled with zero

- Cache pages

- User data pages

- Free pages

In the *Dump Target* window, select the type of the dump target and the URL where you want to save the dump. If you selected a network protocol, such as FTP or SSH, you need to enter relevant access information as well.

Tip: Sharing the Dump Directory with Other Applications

It is possible to specify a path for saving Kdump dumps where other applications also save their dumps. When cleaning its old dump files, Kdump will safely ignore other applications' dump files.

Fill the *Email Notification* window information if you want Kdump to inform you about its events via e-mail and confirm your changes with *OK* after fine tuning Kdump in the *Expert Settings* window. Kdump is now configured.

17.8 Analyzing the Crash Dump

After you obtain the dump, it is time to analyze it. There are several options.

The original tool to analyze the dumps is GDB. You can even use it in the latest environments, although it has several disadvantages and limitations:

- GDB was not specifically designed to debug kernel dumps.

- GDB does not support ELF64 binaries on 32-bit platforms.

- GDB does not understand other formats than ELF dumps (it cannot debug compressed dumps).

That is why the **crash** utility was implemented. It analyzes crash dumps and debugs the running system as well. It provides functionality specific to debugging the Linux kernel and is much more suitable for advanced debugging.

If you want to debug the Linux kernel, you need to install its debugging information package in addition. Check if the package is installed on your system with:

```
tux > zypper se kernel | grep debug
```

 Important: Repository for Packages with Debugging Information

If you subscribed your system for online updates, you can find "debuginfo" packages in the *-Debuginfo-Updates online installation repository relevant for SUSE Linux Enterprise Server 12 SP1. Use YaST to enable the repository.

To open the captured dump in **crash** on the machine that produced the dump, use a command like this:

```
crash /boot/vmlinux-2.6.32.8-0.1-default.gz \
/var/crash/2010-04-23-11\:17/vmcore
```

The first parameter represents the kernel image. The second parameter is the dump file captured by Kdump. You can find this file under /var/crash by default.

Tip: Getting Basic Information from a Kernel Crash Dump

SUSE Linux Enterprise Server ships with the utility `kdumpid` (included in a package with the same name) for identifying unknown kernel dumps. It can be used to extract basic information such as architecture and kernel release. It supports lkcd, diskdump, Kdump files and ELF dumps. When called with the `-v` switch it tries to extract additional information such as machine type, Kernel banner string and Kernel configuration flavor.

17.8.1   Kernel Binary Formats

The Linux kernel comes in Executable and Linkable Format (ELF). This file is usually called `vmlinux` and is directly generated in the compilation process. Not all boot loaders support ELF binaries, especially on the AMD64/Intel 64 architecture. The following solutions exist on different architectures supported by SUSE® Linux Enterprise Server.

17.8.1.1   AMD64/Intel 64

Kernel packages for AMD64/Intel 64 from SUSE contain two kernel files: `vmlinuz` and `vmlinux.gz`.

- `vmlinuz`. This is the file executed by the boot loader.
  The Linux kernel consists of two parts: the kernel itself (`vmlinux`) and the setup code run by the boot loader. These two parts are linked together to create `vmlinuz` (note the distinction: `z` vs. `x`).
  In the kernel source tree, the file is called `bzImage`.

- `vmlinux.gz`. This is a compressed ELF image that can be used by **crash** and GDB. The ELF image is never used by the boot loader itself on AMD64/Intel 64. Therefore, only a compressed version is shipped.

17.8.1.2   POWER

The `yaboot` boot loader on POWER also supports loading ELF images, but not compressed ones. In the POWER kernel package, there is an ELF Linux kernel file `vmlinux`. Considering **crash**, this is the easiest architecture.

If you decide to analyze the dump on another machine, you must check both the architecture of the computer and the files necessary for debugging.

You can analyze the dump on another computer only if it runs a Linux system of the same architecture. To check the compatibility, use the command **uname** -i on both computers and compare the outputs.

If you are going to analyze the dump on another computer, you also need the appropriate files from the kernel and kernel debug packages.

1. Put the kernel dump, the kernel image from /boot, and its associated debugging info file from /usr/lib/debug/boot into a single empty directory.

2. Additionally, copy the kernel modules from /lib/modules/$(uname -r)/kernel/ and the associated debug info files from /usr/lib/debug/lib/modules/$(uname -r)/kernel/ into a subdirectory named modules.

3. In the directory with the dump, the kernel image, its debug info file, and the modules subdirectory, start the **crash** utility:

```
tux > crash vmlinux-version vmcore
```

Regardless of the computer on which you analyze the dump, the crash utility will produce output similar to this:

```
tux > crash /boot/vmlinux-2.6.32.8-0.1-default.gz \
/var/crash/2010-04-23-11\:17/vmcore

crash 4.0-7.6
Copyright (C) 2002, 2003, 2004, 2005, 2006, 2007, 2008  Red Hat, Inc.
Copyright (C) 2004, 2005, 2006  IBM Corporation
Copyright (C) 1999-2006  Hewlett-Packard Co
Copyright (C) 2005, 2006  Fujitsu Limited
Copyright (C) 2006, 2007  VA Linux Systems Japan K.K.
Copyright (C) 2005  NEC Corporation
Copyright (C) 1999, 2002, 2007  Silicon Graphics, Inc.
Copyright (C) 1999, 2000, 2001, 2002  Mission Critical Linux, Inc.
This program is free software, covered by the GNU General Public License,
and you are welcome to change it and/or distribute copies of it under
```

```
certain conditions.  Enter "help copying" to see the conditions.
This program has absolutely no warranty.  Enter "help warranty" for details.


GNU gdb 6.1
Copyright 2004 Free Software Foundation, Inc.
GDB is free software, covered by the GNU General Public License, and you are
welcome to change it and/or distribute copies of it under certain conditions.
Type "show copying" to see the conditions.
There is absolutely no warranty for GDB.  Type "show warranty" for details.
This GDB was configured as "x86_64-unknown-linux-gnu"...


      KERNEL: /boot/vmlinux-2.6.32.8-0.1-default.gz
   DEBUGINFO: /usr/lib/debug/boot/vmlinux-2.6.32.8-0.1-default.debug
    DUMPFILE: /var/crash/2009-04-23-11:17/vmcore
        CPUS: 2
        DATE: Thu Apr 23 13:17:01 2010
      UPTIME: 00:10:41
LOAD AVERAGE: 0.01, 0.09, 0.09
       TASKS: 42
    NODENAME: eros
     RELEASE: 2.6.32.8-0.1-default
     VERSION: #1 SMP 2010-03-31 14:50:44 +0200
     MACHINE: x86_64   (2999 Mhz)
      MEMORY: 1 GB
       PANIC: "SysRq : Trigger a crashdump"
         PID: 9446
     COMMAND: "bash"
        TASK: ffff88003a57c3c0  [THREAD_INFO: ffff880037168000]
         CPU: 1
       STATE: TASK_RUNNING (SYSRQ)
crash>
```

The command output prints first useful data: There were 42 tasks running at the moment of the kernel crash. The cause of the crash was a SysRq trigger invoked by the task with PID 9446. It was a Bash process because the **echo** that has been used is an internal command of the Bash shell.

The **crash** utility builds upon GDB and provides many additional commands. If you enter **bt** without any parameters, the backtrace of the task running at the moment of the crash is printed:

```
crash> bt
PID: 9446    TASK: ffff88003a57c3c0  CPU: 1    COMMAND: "bash"
 #0 [ffff880037169db0] crash_kexec at ffffffff80268fd6
 #1 [ffff880037169e80] __handle_sysrq at ffffffff803d50ed
 #2 [ffff880037169ec0] write_sysrq_trigger at ffffffff802f6fc5
 #3 [ffff880037169ed0] proc_reg_write at ffffffff802f068b
 #4 [ffff880037169f10] vfs_write at ffffffff802b1aba
 #5 [ffff880037169f40] sys_write at ffffffff802b1c1f
 #6 [ffff880037169f80] system_call_fastpath at ffffffff8020bfbb
    RIP: 00007fa958991f60  RSP: 00007fff61330390  RFLAGS: 00010246
    RAX: 0000000000000001  RBX: ffffffff8020bfbb  RCX: 0000000000000001
    RDX: 0000000000000002  RSI: 00007fa959284000  RDI: 0000000000000001
    RBP: 0000000000000002   R8: 00007fa9592516f0   R9: 00007fa958c209c0
    R10: 00007fa958c209c0  R11: 0000000000000246  R12: 00007fa958c1f780
    R13: 00007fa959284000  R14: 0000000000000002  R15: 00000000595569d0
    ORIG_RAX: 0000000000000001  CS: 0033  SS: 002b
crash>
```

Now it is clear what happened: The internal **echo** command of Bash shell sent a character to /proc/sysrq-trigger. After the corresponding handler recognized this character, it invoked the crash_kexec() function. This function called panic() and Kdump saved a dump.

In addition to the basic GDB commands and the extended version of **bt**, the crash utility defines many other commands related to the structure of the Linux kernel. These commands understand the internal data structures of the Linux kernel and present their contents in a human readable format. For example, you can list the tasks running at the moment of the crash with **ps**. With **sym**, you can list all the kernel symbols with the corresponding addresses, or inquire an individual symbol for its value. With **files**, you can display all the open file descriptors of a process. With **kmem**, you can display details about the kernel memory usage. With **vm**, you can inspect the virtual memory of a process, even at the level of individual page mappings. The list of useful commands is very long and many of these accept a wide range of options.

The commands that we mentioned reflect the functionality of the common Linux commands, such as `ps` and `lsof`. If you want to find out the exact sequence of events with the debugger, you need to know how to use GDB and to have strong debugging skills. Both of these are out of the scope of this document. In addition, you need to understand the Linux kernel. Several useful reference information sources are given at the end of this document.

17.9 Advanced Kdump Configuration

The configuration for Kdump is stored in `/etc/sysconfig/kdump`. You can also use YaST to configure it. Kdump configuration options are available under *System › Kernel Kdump* in *YaST Control Center*. The following Kdump options may be useful for you.

You can change the directory for the kernel dumps with the `KDUMP_SAVEDIR` option. Keep in mind that the size of kernel dumps can be very large. Kdump will refuse to save the dump if the free disk space, subtracted by the estimated dump size, drops below the value specified by the `KDUMP_FREE_DISK_SIZE` option. Note that `KDUMP_SAVEDIR` understands the URL format *protocol://specification*, where *protocol* is one of `file`, `ftp`, `sftp`, `nfs` or `cifs`, and `specification` varies for each protocol. For example, to save kernel dump on an FTP server, use the following URL as a template: `ftp://username:password@ftp.example.com:123/var/crash`.

Kernel dumps are usually huge and contain many pages that are not necessary for analysis. With `KDUMP_DUMPLEVEL` option, you can omit such pages. The option understands numeric value between 0 and 31. If you specify *0*, the dump size will be largest. If you specify *31*, it will produce the smallest dump. For a complete table of possible values, see the manual page of **kdump** (`man 7 kdump`).

Sometimes it is very useful to make the size of the kernel dump smaller. For example, if you want to transfer the dump over the network, or if you need to save some disk space in the dump directory. This can be done with `KDUMP_DUMPFORMAT` set to *compressed*. The **crash** utility supports dynamic decompression of the compressed dumps.

> **! Important: Changes to the Kdump Configuration File**
>
> You always need to execute **systemctl restart kdump** after you make manual changes to `/etc/sysconfig/kdump`. Otherwise, these changes will take effect next time you reboot the system.

17.10 For More Information

There is no single comprehensive reference to Kexec and Kdump usage. However, there are helpful resources that deal with certain aspects:

- For the Kexec utility usage, see the manual page of `kexec` (`man 8 kexec`).

- IBM provides a comprehensive documentation on how to use dump tools on the z Systems architecture at http://www.ibm.com/developerworks/linux/linux390/development_documentation.html.

- You can find general information about Kexec at http://www.ibm.com/developerworks/linux/library/l-kexec.html . Might be slightly outdated.

- For more details on Kdump specific to SUSE Linux Enterprise, see http://ftp.suse.com/pub/people/tiwai/kdump-training/kdump-training.pdf .

- An in-depth description of Kdump internals can be found at http://lse.sourceforge.net/kdump/documentation/ols2oo5-kdump-paper.pdf .

For more details on `crash` dump analysis and debugging tools, use the following resources:

- In addition to the info page of GDB (`info gdb`), you might want to read the printable guides at http://sourceware.org/gdb/documentation/ .

- A white paper with a comprehensive description of the crash utility usage can be found at http://people.redhat.com/anderson/crash_whitepaper/.

- The crash utility also features a comprehensive online help. Use `help` *command* to display the online help for `command`.

- If you have the necessary Perl skills, you can use Alicia to make the debugging easier. This Perl-based front-end to the crash utility can be found at http://alicia.sourceforge.net/ .

- If you prefer Python instead, you should install Pykdump. This package helps you control GDB through Python scripts and can be downloaded from http://sf.net/projects/pykdump .

- A very comprehensive overview of the Linux kernel internals is given in *Understanding the Linux Kernel* by Daniel P. Bovet and Marco Cesati (ISBN 978-0-596-00565-8).

VII Synchronized Clocks with Precision Time Protocol

18 Precision Time Protocol

For network environments, it is vital to keep the computer and other devices' clocks synchronized and accurate. There are several solutions to achieve this, for example the widely used Network Time Protocol (NTP) described in *Book "Administration Guide", Chapter 21 "Time Synchronization with NTP"*.

The Precision Time Protocol (PTP) is a protocol capable of sub-microsecond accuracy, which is better than what NTP achieves. PTP support is divided between the kernel and user space. The kernel in SUSE Linux Enterprise Server includes support for PTP clocks, which are provided by network drivers.

18.1 Introduction to PTP

The clocks managed by PTP follow a master-slave hierarchy. The slaves are synchronized to their masters. The hierarchy is updated by the *best master clock* (BMC) algorithm, which runs on every clock. The clock with only one port can be either master or slave. Such a clock is called an *ordinary clock* (OC). A clock with multiple ports can be master on one port and slave on another. Such a clock is called a *boundary clock* (BC). The top-level master is called the *grandmaster clock*. The grandmaster clock can be synchronized with a Global Positioning System (GPS). This way disparate networks can be synchronized with a high degree of accuracy.

The hardware support is the main advantage of PTP. It is supported by various network switches and network interface controllers (NIC). While it is possible to use non-PTP enabled hardware within the network, having network components between all PTP clocks PTP hardware enabled achieves the best possible accuracy.

18.1.1 PTP Linux Implementation

On SUSE Linux Enterprise Server, the implementation of PTP is provided by the `linuxptp` package. Install it with **zypper install linuxptp**. It includes the **ptp4l** and **phc2sys** programs for clock synchronization. **ptp4l** implements the PTP boundary clock and ordinary clock. When hardware time stamping is enabled, **ptp4l** synchronizes the PTP hardware clock to the master clock. With software time stamping, it synchronizes the system clock to the master clock. **phc2sys** is needed only with hardware time stamping to synchronize the system clock to the PTP hardware clock on the network interface card (NIC).

18.2 Using PTP

18.2.1 Network Driver and Hardware Support

PTP requires that the used kernel network driver supports either software or hardware time stamping. Moreover, the NIC must support time stamping in the physical hardware. You can verify the driver and NIC time stamping capabilities with `ethtool`:

```
ethtool -T eth0
Time stamping parameters for eth0:
Capabilities:
hardware-transmit     (SOF_TIMESTAMPING_TX_HARDWARE)
        software-transmit     (SOF_TIMESTAMPING_TX_SOFTWARE)
        hardware-receive      (SOF_TIMESTAMPING_RX_HARDWARE)
        software-receive      (SOF_TIMESTAMPING_RX_SOFTWARE)
        software-system-clock (SOF_TIMESTAMPING_SOFTWARE)
        hardware-raw-clock    (SOF_TIMESTAMPING_RAW_HARDWARE)
PTP Hardware Clock: 0
Hardware Transmit Timestamp Modes:
        off                   (HWTSTAMP_TX_OFF)
        on                    (HWTSTAMP_TX_ON)
Hardware Receive Filter Modes:
        none                  (HWTSTAMP_FILTER_NONE)
        all                   (HWTSTAMP_FILTER_ALL)
```

Software time stamping requires the following parameters:

```
SOF_TIMESTAMPING_SOFTWARE
SOF_TIMESTAMPING_TX_SOFTWARE
SOF_TIMESTAMPING_RX_SOFTWARE
```

Hardware time stamping requires the following parameters:

```
SOF_TIMESTAMPING_RAW_HARDWARE
SOF_TIMESTAMPING_TX_HARDWARE
SOF_TIMESTAMPING_RX_HARDWARE
```

18.2.2 Using **ptp4l**

ptp4l uses hardware time stamping by default. As root, you need to specify the network interface capable of hardware time stamping with the -i option. The -m tells **ptp4l** to print its output to the standard output instead of the system's logging facility:

```
ptp4l -m -i eth0
selected eth0 as PTP clock
port 1: INITIALIZING to LISTENING on INITIALIZE
port 0: INITIALIZING to LISTENING on INITIALIZE
port 1: new foreign master 00a152.fffe.0b334d-1
selected best master clock 00a152.fffe.0b334d
port 1: LISTENING to UNCALIBRATED on RS_SLAVE
master offset -25937 s0 freq +0 path delay      12340
master offset -27887 s0 freq +0 path delay      14232
master offset -38802 s0 freq +0 path delay      13847
master offset -36205 s1 freq +0 path delay      10623
master offset  -6975 s2 freq -30575 path delay  10286
port 1: UNCALIBRATED to SLAVE on MASTER_CLOCK_SELECTED
master offset  -4284 s2 freq -30135 path delay   9892
```

The master offset value represents the measured offset from the master (in nanoseconds).

The s0, s1, s2 indicators show the different states of the clock servo: s0 is unlocked, s1 is clock step, and s2 is locked. If the servo is in the locked state (s2), the clock will not be stepped (only slowly adjusted) if the pi_offset_const option is set to a negative value in the configuration file (see **man 8 ptp4l** for more information).

The freq value represents the frequency adjustment of the clock (in parts per billion, ppb).

The path delay value represents the estimated delay of the synchronization messages sent from the master (in nanoseconds).

Port 0 is a Unix domain socket used for local PTP management. Port 1 is the eth0 interface.

INITIALIZING, LISTENING, UNCALIBRATED and SLAVE are examples of port states which change on INITIALIZE, RS_SLAVE, and MASTER_CLOCK_SELECTED events. When the port state changes from UNCALIBRATED to SLAVE, the computer has successfully synchronized with a PTP master clock.

You can enable software time stamping with the -S option.

```
ptp4l -m -S -i eth3
```

You can also run **ptp4l** as a service:

```
systemctl start ptp4l
```

In this case, **ptp4l** reads its options from the `/etc/sysconfig/ptp4l` file. By default, this file tells **ptp4l** to read the configuration options from `/etc/ptp4l.conf`. For more information on **ptp4l** options and the configuration file settings, see **man 8 ptp4l**.

To enable the **ptp4l** service permanently, run the following:

```
systemctl enable ptp4l
```

To disable it, run

```
systemctl disable ptp4l
```

18.2.3 **ptp4l** Configuration File

ptp4l can read its configuration from an optional configuration file. As no configuration file is used by default, you need to specify it with `-f`.

```
ptp4l -f /etc/ptp4l.conf
```

The configuration file is divided into sections. The global section (indicated as `[global]`) sets the program options, clock options and default port options. Other sections are port specific, and they override the default port options. The name of the section is the name of the configured port —for example, `[eth0]`. An empty port section can be used to replace the command line option.

```
[global]
verbose              1
time_stamping        software
[eth0]
```

The example configuration file is an equivalent of the following command's options:

```
ptp4l -i eth0 -m -S
```

For a complete list of `ptp4l` configuration options, see `man 8 ptp4l`.

18.2.4   Delay Measurement

`ptp4l` measures time delay in two different ways: *peer-to-peer* (P2P) or *end-to-end* (E2E).

P2P

This method is specified with `-P`.

It reacts to changes in the network environment faster and is more accurate in measuring the delay. It is only used in networks where each port exchanges PTP messages with one other port. P2P needs to be supported by all hardware on the communication path.

E2E

This method is specified with `-E`. This is the default.

Automatic method selection

This method is specified with `-A`. The automatic option starts `ptp4l` in E2E mode, and changes to P2P mode if a peer delay request is received.

> ❶ **Important**
>
> All clocks on a single PTP communication path must use the same method to measure the time delay. A warning will be printed if either a peer delay request is received on a port using the E2E mechanism, or an E2E delay request is received on a port using the P2P mechanism.

18.2.5   PTP Management Client: **pmc**

You can use the **pmc** client to obtain more detailed information about `ptp41`. It reads from the standard input—or from the command line—actions specified by name and management ID. Then it sends the actions over the selected transport, and prints any received replies. There are three actions supported: **GET** retrieves the specified information, **SET** updates the specified information, and **CMD** (or **COMMAND**) initiates the specified event.

By default, the management commands are addressed to all ports. The **TARGET** command can be used to select a particular clock and port for the subsequent messages. For a complete list of management IDs, run `pmc help`.

```
pmc -u -b 0 'GET TIME_STATUS_NP'
sending: GET TIME_STATUS_NP
        90f2ca.fffe.20d7e9-0 seq 0 RESPONSE MANAGMENT TIME_STATUS_NP
                master_offset               283
                ingress_time                1361569379345936841
                cumulativeScaledRateOffset  +1.000000000
                scaledLastGmPhaseChange     0
                gmTimeBaseIndicator         0
                lastGmPhaseChange           0x0000'0000000000000000.0000
                gmPresent                   true
                gmIdentity                  00b058.feef.0b448a
```

The `-b` option specifies the boundary hops value in sent messages. Setting it to zero limits the boundary to the local **ptp4l** instance. Increasing the value will retrieve the messages also from PTP nodes that are further from the local instance. The returned information may include:

stepsRemoved

The number of communication nodes to the grandmaster clock.

offsetFromMaster, master_offset

The last measured offset of the clock from the master clock (nanoseconds).

meanPathDelay

The estimated delay of the synchronization messages sent from the master clock (nanoseconds).

gmPresent

If `true`, the PTP clock is synchronized to the master clock; the local clock is not the grandmaster clock.

gmIdentity

This is the grandmaster's identity.

For a complete list of **pmc** command line options, see **man 8 pmc**.

18.3   Synchronizing the Clocks with **phc2sys**

Use **phc2sys** to synchronize the system clock to the PTP hardware clock (PHC) on the network card. The system clock is considered a *slave*, while the network card a *master*. PHC itself is synchronized with **ptp4l** (see *Section 18.2, "Using PTP"*). Use -s to specify the master clock by device or network interface. Use -w to wait until **ptp4l** is in a synchronized state.

```
phc2sys -s eth0 -w
```

PTP operates in *International Atomic Time* (TAI), while the system clock uses *Coordinated Universal Time* (UTC). If you do not specify -w to wait for **ptp4l** synchronization, you can specify the offset in seconds between TAI and UTC with -O :

```
phc2sys -s eth0 -O -35
```

You can run **phc2sys** as a service as well:

```
systemctl start phc2sys
```

In this case, **phc2sys** reads its options from the /etc/sysconfig/phc2sys file. For more information on **phc2sys** options, see **man 8 phc2sys** .

To enable the **phc2sys** service permanently, run the following:

```
systemctl enable phc2sys
```

To disable it, run

```
systemctl dosable phc2sys
```

18.3.1   Verifying Time Synchronization

When PTP time synchronization is working properly and hardware time stamping is used, **ptp4l** and **phc2sys** output messages with time offsets and frequency adjustments periodically to the system log.

An example of the **ptp4l** output:

```
ptp4l[351.358]: selected /dev/ptp0 as PTP clock
```

```
ptp4l[352.361]: port 1: INITIALIZING to LISTENING on INITIALIZE
ptp4l[352.361]: port 0: INITIALIZING to LISTENING on INITIALIZE
ptp4l[353.210]: port 1: new foreign master 00a069.eefe.0b442d-1
ptp4l[357.214]: selected best master clock 00a069.eefe.0b662d
ptp4l[357.214]: port 1: LISTENING to UNCALIBRATED on RS_SLAVE
ptp4l[359.224]: master offset       3304 s0 freq      +0 path delay     9202
ptp4l[360.224]: master offset       3708 s1 freq  -28492 path delay     9202
ptp4l[361.224]: master offset      -3145 s2 freq  -32637 path delay     9202
ptp4l[361.224]: port 1: UNCALIBRATED to SLAVE on MASTER_CLOCK_SELECTED
ptp4l[362.223]: master offset       -145 s2 freq  -30580 path delay     9202
ptp4l[363.223]: master offset       1043 s2 freq  -28436 path delay     8972
[...]
ptp4l[371.235]: master offset        285 s2 freq  -28511 path delay     9199
ptp4l[372.235]: master offset        -78 s2 freq  -28788 path delay     9204
```

An example of the **phc2sys** output:

```
phc2sys[616.617]: Waiting for ptp4l...
phc2sys[628.628]: phc offset      66341 s0 freq      +0 delay   2729
phc2sys[629.628]: phc offset      64668 s1 freq  -37690 delay   2726
[...]
phc2sys[646.630]: phc offset       -333 s2 freq  -37426 delay   2747
phc2sys[646.630]: phc offset        194 s2 freq  -36999 delay   2749
```

ptp4l normally writes messages very frequently. You can reduce the frequency with the summary_interval directive. Its value is an exponent of the 2^N expression. For example, to reduce the output to every 1024 (which equals to 2^10) seconds, add the following line to the /etc/ptp4l.conf file:

```
summary_interval 10
```

You can also reduce the frequency of the **phc2sys** command's updates with the -u *summary-updates* option.

18.4 Examples of Configurations

This section includes several examples of **ptp4l** configuration. The examples are not full configuration files but rather minimal list of changes to be done to the specific files. The string *ethX* stands for the actual network interface name in your setup.

EXAMPLE 18.1: SLAVE CLOCK USING SOFTWARE TIME STAMPING

`/etc/sysconfig/ptp4l`:

```
OPTIONS="-f /etc/ptp4l.conf -i ethX"
```

No changes made to the distribution `/etc/ptp4l.conf`.

EXAMPLE 18.2: SLAVE CLOCK USING HARDWARE TIME STAMPING

`/etc/sysconfig/ptp4l`:

```
OPTIONS="-f /etc/ptp4l.conf -i ethX"
```

`/etc/sysconfig/phc2sys`:

```
OPTIONS="-s ethX -w"
```

No changes made to the distribution `/etc/ptp4l.conf`.

EXAMPLE 18.3: MASTER CLOCK USING HARDWARE TIME STAMPING

`/etc/sysconfig/ptp4l`:

```
OPTIONS="-f /etc/ptp4l.conf -i ethX"
```

`/etc/sysconfig/phc2sys`:

```
OPTIONS="-s CLOCK_REALTIME -c ethX -w"
```

`/etc/ptp4l.conf`:

```
priority1 127
```

EXAMPLE 18.4: MASTER CLOCK USING SOFTWARE TIME STAMPING (NOT GENERALLY RECOMMENDED)

`/etc/sysconfig/ptp4l`:

```
OPTIONS="-f /etc/ptp4l.conf -i ethX"
```

```
/etc/ptp4l.conf:
```

```
priority1 127
```

18.5   PTP and NTP

NTP and PTP time synchronization tools can coexist, synchronizing time from one to another in both directions.

18.5.1   NTP to PTP Synchronization

When `ntpd` is used to synchronize the local system clock, you can configure the **ptp4l** to be the grandmaster clock distributing the time from the local system clock via PTP. Include the `priority1` option in `/etc/ptp4l.conf`:

```
[global]
priority1 127
[eth0]
```

Then run **ptp4l**:

```
ptp4l -f /etc/ptp4l.conf
```

When hardware time stamping is used, you need to synchronize the PTP hardware clock to the system clock with **phc2sys**:

```
phc2sys -c eth0 -s CLOCK_REALTIME -w
```

18.5.2   PTP to NTP Synchronization

You can configure `ntpd` to distribute the time from the system clock synchronized by **ptp4l** or **phc2sys** by using the *local* reference clock driver. Moreover, you need to stop `ntpd` from adjusting the system clock—do not specify any remote NTP servers in `/etc/ntp.conf`:

```
server   127.127.1.0
```

```
fudge    127.127.1.0 stratum 0
```

 Note: NTP and DHCP

When the DHCP client command **dhclient** receives a list of NTP servers, it adds them to NTP configuration by default. To prevent this behavior, set

```
NETCONFIG_NTP_POLICY=""
```

in the /etc/sysconfig/network/config file.

A Documentation Updates

This chapter lists content changes for this document.

This manual was updated on the following dates:

A.1 December 2015 (Initial Release of SUSE Linux Enterprise Server 12 SP1)

General

- *Book "Subscription Management Tool for SLES 12 SP1"* is now part of the documentation for SUSE Linux Enterprise Server.

- Add-ons provided by SUSE have been renamed to modules and extensions. The manuals have been updated to reflect this change.

- Numerous small fixes and additions to the documentation, based on technical feedback.

- The registration service has been changed from Novell Customer Center to SUSE Customer Center.

- In YaST, you will now reach *Network Settings* via the *System* group. *Network Devices* is gone (https://bugzilla.suse.com/show_bug.cgi?id=867809).

- **Added** *Section 2.5.2, " Show the Network Usage of Processes:* `nethogs` *"* (Fate #313501).

- **Added** Perf chapter, including introductory information about Instruction-Based Sampling (IBS) (Fate #315868).

- **Added** PTP chapter (Fate #316795).

Bugfixes

- **Removed** obsolete `acpid.service` (https://bugzilla.suse.com/show_bug.cgi?id=918655).

- *Section 2.4.2, "Detailed Memory Usage:* `/proc/meminfo`*"*: **Expanded** information on `/proc/meminfo` (https://bugzilla.suse.com/show_bug.cgi?id=926521).

- *Chapter 9, Kernel Control Groups*: **General** **Update** (Fate #312101 and https://bugzilla.suse.com/show_bug.cgi?id=897313).

- *Section 12.2.2, "*`NOOP`*"*: **Added** recommendation for `NOOP` in multipathing environments (Fate #319091).

- *Section 17.4, "Calculating* `crashkernel` *Allocation Size"*: **Updated** `crashkernel` allocation recommendations (https://bugzilla.suse.com/show_bug.cgi?id=948565 and https://bugzilla.suse.com/show_bug.cgi?id=948954).

A.2   February 2015 (Documentation Maintenance Update)

Bugfixes

- *Section 12.2, "Available I/O Elevators"*: **Increasing** individual thread throughput using CFQ on SLE 12 (https://bugzilla.suse.com/show_bug.cgi?id=907506).

- *Section 14.3.2, "Writeback Parameters"*: **Important** difference in timing of I/O writes in SLE 12 (https://bugzilla.suse.com/show_bug.cgi?id=907504).

A.3 October 2014 (Initial Release of SUSE Linux Enterprise Server 12)

General

- Removed all KDE documentation and references because KDE is no longer shipped.

- Removed all references to SuSEconfig, which is no longer supported (Fate #100011).

- Move from System V init to systemd (Fate #310421). Updated affected parts of the documentation.

- YaST Runlevel Editor has changed to Services Manager (Fate #312568). Updated affected parts of the documentation.

- Removed all references to ISDN support, as ISDN support has been removed (Fate #314594).

- Removed all references to the YaST DSL module as it is no longer shipped (Fate #316264).

- Removed all references to the YaST Modem module as it is no longer shipped (Fate #316264).

- Btrfs has become the default file system for the root partition (Fate #315901). Updated affected parts of the documentation.

- The `dmesg` now provides human-readable time stamps in `ctime()`-like format (Fate #316056). Updated affected parts of the documentation.

- syslog and syslog-ng have been replaced by rsyslog (Fate #316175). Updated affected parts of the documentation.

- MariaDB is now shipped as the relational database instead of MySQL (Fate #313595). Updated affected parts of the documentation.

- SUSE-related products are no longer available from http://download.novell.com but from http://download.suse.com. Adjusted links accordingly.

- Novell Customer Center has been replaced with SUSE Customer Center. Updated affected parts of the documentation.

- `/var/run` is mounted as tmpfs (Fate #303793). Updated affected parts of the documentation.

- The following architectures are no longer supported: Itanium and x86. Updated affected parts of the documentation.

- The traditional method for setting up the network with `ifconfig` has been replaced by `wicked`. Updated affected parts of the documentation.

- A lot of networking commands are deprecated and have been replaced by newer commands (usually **ip**). Updated affected parts of the documentation.

```
arp: ip neighbor
ifconfig: ip addr, ip link
iptunnel: ip tunnel
iwconfig: iw
nameif: ip link, ifrename
netstat: ss, ip route, ip -s link, ip maddr
route: ip route
```

- Numerous small fixes and additions to the documentation, based on technical feedback.

Chapter 2, System Monitoring Utilities

- Updated command outputs with samples produced with SUSE Linux Enterprise 12.

- Corrected the description of `si`, `so` and `in` in *Section 2.1.1, "vmstat"*.

- Corrected the explanation for `majflt` and the statement about spreading I/O requests over multiple disks in *Section 2.1.2.1, "Generating reports with sar"*.

- Replaced deprecated tools **ifconfig** and **netstat** with **ip**, **ethtool** and **ss** in *Section 2.5, "Networking"*.

- Added documentation about **sysctl** to *Section 2.6.2, "System Control Parameters: / proc/sys/"*.

- Added the section *Section 2.7.3, "MCELog: Machine Check Exceptions (MCE)"*.

- Added details on **/usr/bin/time** to *Section 2.10.1, "Time Measurement with time"*.

Chapter 4, SystemTap—Filtering and Analyzing System Data

Added a link to the example scripts Web page to *Section 4.1.1, "SystemTap Scripts"*.

Chapter 7, OProfile—System-Wide Profiler

Corrected statements on the effects of sampling rates in *Section 7.4.2, "Getting Event Configurations"*.

Chapter 10, Automatic Non-Uniform Memory Access (NUMA) Balancing

New chapter.

Chapter 13, Tuning the Task Scheduler

- Removed section about the outdated O1 task scheduler.

- Clarified kernel variables in *Section 14.1.5, "Writeback"*.

Chapter 14, Tuning the Memory Management Subsystem

Added detailed descriptions on tunable parameters to *Section 14.3.2, "Writeback Parameters"*.

Chapter 17, Kexec and Kdump

- Added a tip on sharing the dump directory in *Section 17.7.2, "YaST Configuration"* (Fate #313185).

- Added a tip on identifying a Kernel crash dump with `kdumpid` (Fate #312855) to *Section 17.8, "Analyzing the Crash Dump"*.

Obsolete Content

- Chapter *Monitoring with Nagios* has been removed from *Part II, "System Monitoring"* (Fate #316136), because Nagios is no longer shipped on SUSE Linux Enterprise 12.

- Chapter *Perfmon2—Hardware-Based Performance Monitoring* has been removed from *Part III, "Kernel Monitoring"*, because perfmon2 is no longer shipped on SUSE Linux Enterprise 12.

Bugfixes

- Removed notes about `zone_reclaim_mode` in *Chapter 14, Tuning the Memory Management Subsystem* (https://bugzilla.suse.com/show_bug.cgi?id=874971).

B GNU Licenses

This appendix contains the GNU Free Documentation License version 1.2.

GNU Free Documentation License

Copyright (C) 2000, 2001, 2002 Free Software Foundation, Inc. 51 Franklin St, Fifth Floor, Boston, MA 02110-1301 USA. Everyone is permitted to copy and distribute verbatim copies of this license document, but changing it is not allowed.

0. PREAMBLE

The purpose of this License is to make a manual, textbook, or other functional and useful document "free" in the sense of freedom: to assure everyone the effective freedom to copy and redistribute it, with or without modifying it, either commercially or non-commercially. Secondarily, this License preserves for the author and publisher a way to get credit for their work, while not being considered responsible for modifications made by others.

This License is a kind of "copyleft", which means that derivative works of the document must themselves be free in the same sense. It complements the GNU General Public License, which is a copyleft license designed for free software.

We have designed this License to use it for manuals for free software, because free software needs free documentation: a free program should come with manuals providing the same freedoms that the software does. But this License is not limited to software manuals; it can be used for any textual work, regardless of subject matter or whether it is published as a printed book. We recommend this License principally for works whose purpose is instruction or reference.

1. APPLICABILITY AND DEFINITIONS

This License applies to any manual or other work, in any medium, that contains a notice placed by the copyright holder saying it can be distributed under the terms of this License. Such a notice grants a world-wide, royalty-free license, unlimited in duration, to use that work under the conditions stated herein. The "Document", below, refers to any such manual or work. Any member of the public is a licensee, and is addressed as "you". You accept the license if you copy, modify or distribute the work in a way requiring permission under copyright law.

A "Modified Version" of the Document means any work containing the Document or a portion of it, either copied verbatim, or with modifications and/or translated into another language.

A "Secondary Section" is a named appendix or a front-matter section of the Document that deals exclusively with the relationship of the publishers or authors of the Document to the Document's overall subject (or to related matters) and contains nothing that could fall directly within that overall subject. (Thus, if the Document is in part a textbook of mathematics, a Secondary Section may not explain any mathematics.) The relationship could be a matter of historical connection with the subject or with related matters, or of legal, commercial, philosophical, ethical or political position regarding them.

The "Invariant Sections" are certain Secondary Sections whose titles are designated, as being those of Invariant Sections, in the notice that says that the Document is released under this License. If a section does not fit the above definition of Secondary then it is not allowed to be designated as Invariant. The Document may contain zero Invariant Sections. If the Document does not identify any Invariant Sections then there are none.

The "Cover Texts" are certain short passages of text that are listed, as Front-Cover Texts or Back-Cover Texts, in the notice that says that the Document is released under this License. A Front-Cover Text may be at most 5 words, and a Back-Cover Text may be at most 25 words.

A "Transparent" copy of the Document means a machine-readable copy, represented in a format whose specification is available to the general public, that is suitable for revising the document straightforwardly with generic text editors or (for images composed of pixels) generic paint programs or (for drawings) some widely available draw-ing editor, and that is suitable for input to text formatters or for automatic translation to a variety of formats suitable for input to text formatters. A copy made in an otherwise Transparent file format whose markup, or absence of markup, has been arranged to thwart or discourage subsequent modification by readers is not Transparent. An image format is not Transparent if used for any substantial amount of text. A copy that is not "Transparent" is called "Opaque".

Examples of suitable formats for Transparent copies include plain ASCII without markup, Texinfo input format, LaTeX input format, SGML or XML using a publicly available DTD, and standard-conforming simple HTML, PostScript or PDF designed for human modification. Examples of transparent image formats include PNG, XCF and JPG. Opaque formats include proprietary formats that can be read and edited only by proprietary word processors, SGML or XML for which the DTD and/or processing tools are not generally available, and the machine-generated HTML, PostScript or PDF produced by some word processors for output purposes only.

The "Title Page" means, for a printed book, the title page itself, plus such following pages as are needed to hold, legibly, the material this License requires to appear in the title page. For works in formats which do not have any title page as such, "Title Page" means the text near the most prominent appearance of the work's title, preceding the beginning of the body of the text.

A section "Entitled XYZ" means a named subunit of the Document whose title either is precisely XYZ or contains XYZ in parentheses following text that translates XYZ in another language. (Here XYZ stands for a specific section name mentioned below, such as "Acknowledgements", "Dedications", "Endorsements", or "History".) To "Preserve the Title" of such a section when you modify the Document means that it remains a section "Entitled XYZ" according to this definition.

The Document may include Warranty Disclaimers next to the notice which states that this License applies to the Document. These Warranty Disclaimers are considered to be included by reference in this License, but only as regards disclaiming warranties: any other implication that these Warranty Disclaimers may have is void and has no effect on the meaning of this License.

2. VERBATIM COPYING

You may copy and distribute the Document in any medium, either commercially or noncommercially, provided that this License, the copyright notices, and the license notice saying this License applies to the Document are reproduced in all copies, and that you add no other conditions whatsoever to those of this License. You may not use technical measures to obstruct or control the reading or further copying of the copies you make or distribute. However, you may accept compensation in exchange for copies. If you distribute a large enough number of copies you must also follow the conditions in section 3.

You may also lend copies, under the same conditions stated above, and you may publicly display copies.

3. COPYING IN QUANTITY

If you publish printed copies (or copies in media that commonly have printed covers) of the Document, numbering more than 100, and the Document's license notice requires Cover Texts, you must enclose the copies in covers that carry, clearly and legibly, all these Cover Texts: Front-Cover Texts on the front cover, and Back-Cover Texts on the back cover. Both covers must also clearly and legibly identify you as the publisher of these copies. The front cover must present the full title with all words of the title equally prominent and visible. You may add other material on the covers in addition. Copying with changes limited to the covers, as long as they preserve the title of the Document and satisfy these conditions, can be treated as verbatim copying in other respects.

If the required texts for either cover are too voluminous to fit legibly, you should put the first ones listed (as many as fit reasonably) on the actual cover, and continue the rest onto adjacent pages.

If you publish or distribute Opaque copies of the Document numbering more than 100, you must either include a machine-readable Transparent copy along with each Opaque copy, or state in or with each Opaque copy a computer-network location from which the general network-using public has access to download using public-standard network protocols a complete Transparent copy of the Document, free of added material. If you use the latter option, you must take reasonably prudent steps, when you begin distribution of Opaque copies in quantity, to ensure that this Transparent copy will remain thus accessible at the stated location until at least one year after the last time you distribute an Opaque copy (directly or through your agents or retailers) of that edition to the public.

It is requested, but not required, that you contact the authors of the Document well before redistributing any large number of copies, to give them a chance to provide you with an updated version of the Document.

4. MODIFICATIONS

You may copy and distribute a Modified Version of the Document under the conditions of sections 2 and 3 above, provided that you release the Modified Version under precisely this License, with the Modified Version filling the role of the Document, thus licensing distribution and modification of the Modified Version to whoever possesses a copy of it. In addition, you must do these things in the Modified Version:

A. Use in the Title Page (and on the covers, if any) a title distinct from that of the Document, and from those of previous versions (which should, if there were any, be listed in the History section of the Document). You may use the same title as a previous version if the original publisher of that version gives permission.

B. List on the Title Page, as authors, one or more persons or entities responsible for authorship of the modifications in the Modified Version, together with at least five of the principal authors of the Document (all of its principal authors, if it has fewer than five), unless they release you from this requirement.

C. State on the Title page the name of the publisher of the Modified Version, as the publisher.

D. Preserve all the copyright notices of the Document.

E. Add an appropriate copyright notice for your modifications adjacent to the other copyright notices.

F. Include, immediately after the copyright notices, a license notice giving the public permission to use the Modified Version under the terms of this License, in the form shown in the Addendum below.

G. Preserve in that license notice the full lists of Invariant Sections and required Cover Texts given in the Document's license notice.

H. Include an unaltered copy of this License.

I. Preserve the section Entitled "History", Preserve its Title, and add to it an item stating at least the title, year, new authors, and publisher of the Modified Version as given on the Title Page. If there is no section Entitled "History" in the Document, create one stating the title, year, authors, and publisher of the Document as given on its Title Page, then add an item describing the Modified Version as stated in the previous sentence.

J. Preserve the network location, if any, given in the Document for public access to a Transparent copy of the Document, and likewise the network locations given in the Document for previous versions it was based on. These may be placed in the "History" section. You may omit a network location for a work that was published at least four years before the Document itself, or if the original publisher of the version it refers to gives permission.

K. For any section Entitled "Acknowledgements" or "Dedications", Preserve the Title of the section, and preserve in the section all the substance and tone of each of the contributor acknowledgements and/or dedications given therein.

L. Preserve all the Invariant Sections of the Document, unaltered in their text and in their titles. Section numbers or the equivalent are not considered part of the section titles.

M. Delete any section Entitled "Endorsements". Such a section may not be included in the Modified Version.

N. Do not retitle any existing section to be Entitled "Endorsements" or to conflict in title with any Invariant Section.

O. Preserve any Warranty Disclaimers.

If the Modified Version includes new front-matter sections or appendices that qualify as Secondary Sections and contain no material copied from the Document, you may at your option designate some or all of these sections as invariant. To do this, add their titles to the list of Invariant Sections in the Modified Version's license notice. These titles must be distinct from any other section titles.

You may add a section Entitled "Endorsements", provided it contains nothing but endorsements of your Modified Version by various parties--for example, statements of peer review or that the text has been approved by an organization as the authoritative definition of a standard.

You may add a passage of up to five words as a Front-Cover Text, and a passage of up to 25 words as a Back-Cover Text, to the end of the list of Cover Texts in the Modified Version. Only one passage of Front-Cover Text and one of Back-Cover Text may be added by (or through arrangements made by) any one entity. If the Document already includes a cover text for the same cover, previously added by you or by arrangement made by the same entity you are acting on behalf of, you may not add another; but you may replace the old one, on explicit permission from the previous publisher that added the old one.

The author(s) and publisher(s) of the Document do not by this License give permission to use their names for publicity for or to assert or imply endorsement of any Modified Version.

5. COMBINING DOCUMENTS

You may combine the Document with other documents released under this License, under the terms defined in section 4 above for modified versions, provided that you include in the combination all of the Invariant Sections of all of the original documents, unmodified, and list them all as Invariant Sections of your combined work in its license notice, and that you preserve all their Warranty Disclaimers.

The combined work need only contain one copy of this License, and multiple identical Invariant Sections may be replaced with a single copy. If there are multiple Invariant Sections with the same name but different contents, make the title of each such section unique by adding at the end of it, in parentheses, the name of the original author or publisher of that section if known, or else a unique number. Make the same adjustment to the section titles in the list of Invariant Sections in the license notice of the combined work.

In the combination, you must combine any sections Entitled "History" in the various original documents, forming one section Entitled "History"; likewise combine any sections Entitled "Acknowledgements", and any sections Entitled "Dedications". You must delete all sections Entitled "Endorsements".

6. COLLECTIONS OF DOCUMENTS

You may make a collection consisting of the Document and other documents released under this License, and replace the individual copies of this License in the various documents with a single copy that is included in the collection, provided that you follow the rules of this License for verbatim copying of each of the documents in all other respects.

You may extract a single document from such a collection, and distribute it individually under this License, provided you insert a copy of this License into the extracted document, and follow this License in all other respects regarding verbatim copying of that document.

7. AGGREGATION WITH INDEPENDENT WORKS

A compilation of the Document or its derivatives with other separate and independent documents or works, in or on a volume of a storage or distribution medium, is called an "aggregate" if the copyright resulting from the compilation is not used to limit the legal rights of the compilation's users beyond what the individual works permit. When the Document is included in an aggregate, this License does not apply to the other works in the aggregate which are not themselves derivative works of the Document.

If the Cover Text requirement of section 3 is applicable to these copies of the Document, then if the Document is less than one half of the entire aggregate, the Document's Cover Texts may be placed on covers that bracket the Document within the aggregate, or the electronic equivalent of covers if the Document is in electronic form. Otherwise they must appear on printed covers that bracket the whole aggregate.

8. TRANSLATION

Translation is considered a kind of modification, so you may distribute translations of the Document under the terms of section 4. Replacing Invariant Sections with translations requires special permission from their copyright holders, but you may include translations of some or all Invariant Sections in addition to the original versions of these Invariant Sections. You may include a translation of this License, and all the license notices in the Document, and any Warranty Disclaimers, provided that you also include the original English version of this License and the original versions of those notices and disclaimers. In case of a disagreement between the translation and the original version of this License or a notice or disclaimer, the original version will prevail.

If a section in the Document is Entitled "Acknowledgements", "Dedications", or "History", the requirement (section 4) to Preserve its Title (section 1) will typically require changing the actual title.

9. TERMINATION

You may not copy, modify, sublicense, or distribute the Document except as expressly provided for under this License. Any other attempt to copy, modify, sublicense or distribute the Document is void, and will automatically terminate your rights under this License. However, parties who have received copies, or rights, from you under this License will not have their licenses terminated so long as such parties remain in full compliance.

10. FUTURE REVISIONS OF THIS LICENSE

The Free Software Foundation may publish new, revised versions of the GNU Free Documentation License from time to time. Such new versions will be similar in spirit to the present version, but may differ in detail to address new problems or concerns. See http://www.gnu.org/copyleft/.

Each version of the License is given a distinguishing version number. If the Document specifies that a particular numbered version of this License "or any later version" applies to it, you have the option of following the terms and conditions either of that specified version or of any later version that has been published (not as a draft) by the Free Software Foundation. If the Document does not specify a version number of this License, you may choose any version ever published (not as a draft) by the Free Software Foundation.

ADDENDUM: How to use this License for your documents

```
Copyright (c) YEAR YOUR NAME.

Permission is granted to copy, distribute and/or modify this document

under the terms of the GNU Free Documentation License, Version 1.2

or any later version published by the Free Software Foundation;

with no Invariant Sections, no Front-Cover Texts, and no Back-Cover

 Texts.

A copy of the license is included in the section entitled "GNU

Free Documentation License".
```

If you have Invariant Sections, Front-Cover Texts and Back-Cover Texts, replace the "with...Texts." line with this:

```
with the Invariant Sections being LIST THEIR TITLES, with the

Front-Cover Texts being LIST, and with the Back-Cover Texts being LIST.
```

If you have Invariant Sections without Cover Texts, or some other combination of the three, merge those two alternatives to suit the situation.

If your document contains nontrivial examples of program code, we recommend releasing these examples in parallel under your choice of free software license, such as the GNU General Public License, to permit their use in free software.